*To Craig, Grant, and Connor,
with love and thankfulness*

# CONTENTS

# TRANSFORMED

## *not* CONFORMED

Blessings!
Missy
Emerson

# TRANSFORMED

*not* CONFORMED

*Embracing a Life-Changing Approach*
*to Spiritual Habits*

## MISSY EVERSOLE

ISBN 13: 978-1-64645-256-9 (Paperback)
978-1-64645-257-6 (ePub)
978-1-64645-258-3 (Mobi)

Library of Congress Catalog Card Number: 2021908640

# ACKNOWLEDGMENTS

This book that you are holding in your hands or reading on your electronic device is one of blood, sweat, and tears—a lot of tears! When the Lord called me to step out in faith and write this book, I knew I needed all the prayers and support I could get. When fear and doubt crept in, my prayer warriors and encouragers lifted me up in prayer.

Thank you to my prayer team Jackie Fritz, Jenny Friday, Laura Hinchman, Rhoda Kennell, and Lauren Sarnacki. Your prayers and encouraging texts got me through this journey!

Thank you, Tracy Mann, for your support, words of encouragement, prayers, and friendship. At the beginning of this process, you asked me, "When are you going to start calling yourself a writer? Because you are!" I can now finally answer this question with confidence. I am a writer!

Thank you, Ginger Bachman, for your friendship, prayers, and laughter. Our banter back and forth made my day! Thank you for caring for my boys when they needed some extra support at school. Enjoy your retirement; you deserve it, my friend!

Thank you to my coworkers at Peoria Christian School. Your prayers and support mean the world to me.

Thank you to my Compel Critique Group: Ann, Audrey, Charlene, Lori, Molly, and Standra. We are a group of writers from different backgrounds and different parts of the US and Canada, but we are each other's biggest cheerleaders. Thank you for your input and suggestions throughout this whole writing process.

Thank you to my writing coach, Jeanette Hanscome. It was a joy working with you as I saw this dream of writing a book become a reality.

Thank you, Ann Swindell, for accepting me into your "Writing with Grace" mastermind group in August 2019. The spark that lit the fire for this book originated from being in this group. Thank you for your words of encouragement and suggestions as you read some of the early sections of this book.

Thank you, Grant and Connor, for your love and support. I am so blessed to be your mom. I thank God every day for you, and I am so proud of you both. You are my light in the darkest days! As you grow older and start to leave the nest, please know that I love and support you in whatever you do, and I will never stop praying for you!

Thank you, Craig. I'm in tears as I write this because I honestly don't know where to begin. You have always been my biggest cheerleader and supporter. When I don't think I can do anymore, you give me the strength to take that next step. You, Grant, and Connor are my world, and I love you all so much!

# PART 1

## COMING
## FULL CIRCLE

*Therefore, if anyone is in Christ,*
*he is a new creation.*
*The old has passed away; behold,*
*the new has come.*
2 Corinthians 5:17

# *CHAPTER 1*

TRANSFORMING,
NOT CONFORMING

*Do not be conformed to this world,*
*but be transformed by the renewal of your mind,*
*that by testing you may discern what is the will of God,*
*what is good and acceptable and perfect.*
Romans 12:2

## Pinterest Perfect

Stuck between the perfect Pinterest life, a messy house, and a chaotic schedule is a woman who needs a reminder that she is the daughter of the King. She is a royal princess who *sees* the immense love for her flowing through the pages of her well-worn Bible but at times cannot *feel* that love.

Reflecting on the early days of her relationship with Christ, she remembers a woman eager to dig into her newly purchased NIV Bible, its pages crisp and clean. The verses lined the pages with purple ink, symbolic of the royal family she now belonged to.

Over time, her life's priorities replaced her desire to learn more about her Savior. Diaper changes, late-night feedings, and sporadic catnaps replaced the Bible she once held in her hands with the eagerness to study more about the sacrificial love of Christ.

Responding to the Lord's call, she invested all her time raising her children in a loving, Christian home. She did all the things that a "good Christian woman" was expected to do. She attended church weekly, participated in Bible studies, and volunteered in the church nursery. On the outside, she looked put together, but she was a train wreck on the inside. She grumbled about serving. She only opened her Bible on Sundays. And that weekly Bible study that she attended so faithfully? About an hour before the scheduled time to meet, she quickly filled in the blanks to make it appear that she studied daily and faithfully throughout the week.

Throughout this season of her life, she pondered the same question over and over . . .

*Where is the fire that I once had for Christ?*

"Maybe I will find it when the boys get into school? Yes, that's when I will be able to devote more time to the Lord. After all, the Lord gave me these children to raise, so my main focus right now needs to be on them." She mistakenly thought there would be plenty of time to study the Bible and spend time with Him after her boys got into school.

Instead of devoting time to the Lord, she focused on her earthly identities, which came in the forms of a wife, mom, coworker, daughter, volunteer, ministry leader, and whatever else came along that demanded attention.

She took pride in her earthly identities and devoted 110 percent to them. Exhausted by the end of the day due to her endless commitments, she often crawled into bed in tears. She had a loving and supportive family, but something was missing in her life. Running on empty, fueled by unhealthy eating habits and caffeine, she found herself short and snippy with her family. Her husband did nothing right in her mind, and her children, doing what normal children do, were too loud and didn't listen.

Fully believing her family were the ones who needed to change, she overlooked her faults. It was easy to blame her family for her stress until her actions in the middle school parking lot revealed she was the one at fault. Etched in her mind forever are her actions, the defeated look on her children's faces, and the stares from other parents.

Defeated and desperate for a change, she asks herself again, *Where is the fire I once had for Christ?*

She didn't realize it yet, but there was hope, and it was within her reach. In fact, she had been carrying it around with her every day. She just needed to dig a little deeper to grasp on to it. Once she took hold of it, her soul would reawaken and reignite the fire for Christ that she once had all those years ago.

That hope was contained in the Bible, the living Word. Throughout the New Testament were reminders of who she is in Christ. As she began to read the living water of the Word of God, suddenly her tiredness and spiritual drought were being replenished. The spiritual practices that she began to implement in her life have since had a significant impact on her.

## You Are Not Alone

I am this woman, and if you are reading this book, I suspect your current situation is like what I have described. The pressures of the world's expectations lie on your shoulders, and those expectations replaced the fire you once had for Christ. In the eyes of the social media world, there is a certain way to raise your children, keep your home clean, and prepare a dinner that comes from all-organic food. It's exhausting to try and keep up with the demands that social media enforces on us.

Have you ever wondered what would happen if you set aside the pressures of the world and focused back on the time when you first became a believer? Take a moment to reflect on when you accepted Christ as your Savior. Remember the craving to soak up the Word of God? Remember opening your Bible for the first time and reading the words that would bring you comfort in times of happiness, sadness, or despair? Remember the newness of it?

I have found that when I am exhausted by the world's demands, my soul is experiencing a spiritual drought. I'm sure you feel the same way.

## A Journey of Hills and Valleys

From the moment we accepted Christ as our Lord and Savior, we've been on a spiritual transformation journey. The apostle Paul writes in 2 Corinthians 5:17, "Therefore, if anyone is in Christ, he is a new creation. The old has passed away; behold, the new has come."

*If you are in Christ, you are a new creation.* What a beautiful description of our new relationship with Christ. We are one with Him, and our past, our hurts, and our failures are forgiven and gone. We are a new creation. While not a physical presence, we can be attentive to Christ's spiritual presence when we are in the right frame of mind.

While Christ is in us, this doesn't mean life will be all fine and dandy. We all have been through challenging times. Times when we didn't even have the strength to get out of bed. Times when we questioned if God was truly with us and heard our cries.

Is your spiritual journey like mine? One moment, I am white-hot and on fire for the Lord, and the next thing I know, I am lukewarm and going through the motions. At times I've felt so close to Jesus I could feel His heart beating. "He will cover you with his feathers. He will shelter you with his wings. His faithful promises are your armor and protection" (Psalm 91:4 NLT). Other times I've been so deep in the dark pit of sin that the enemy convinced me I was no longer loved and was alone in my despair because of those sins.

Can you relate to this? Looking over your life, what hills and valleys have you gone through? Perhaps, you are in a valley now, and you are grasping to climb out but feel hopeless, not knowing where to even begin. Or maybe you are on the hill but are yearning for more—to draw closer to Christ and leave worldly thoughts and opinions behind.

What would you say if I told you that you can reignite your love for Christ? No matter all you've been through, the Lord is waiting with open arms.

Thankfully, the Lord provides us with the disciplines and tools needed to draw closer to Him. These tools are practices or habits that you may be doing every day while not even realizing it.

# CHAPTER 2

## FOR SUCH A TIME AS THIS—
## WHY SPIRITUAL HABITS
## ARE IMPORTANT

*And I am sure of this,*
*that he who began a good work in you*
*will bring it to completion*
*at the day of Jesus Christ.*
Philippians 1:6

You may be asking what exactly are these disciplines, or what I like to call habits. At first glance, spiritual discipline sounds like a rigorous technique that only monks in an isolated chapel high in the mountains would participate in. Or perhaps, your view about spiritual disciplines is something that only profound theologians practice, not women who are deep into raising their children or grandchildren, managing their household, working full-time, volunteering, and doing whatever else the world throws at them.

The word *discipline* sounds like we are being forced to do it. On the other hand, the word *habit* sounds like something we are willingly doing. As a strong-willed, somewhat stubborn person, I am more likely to engage in something I want to do than what I am forced to do.

A quick Google search of "What are the spiritual disciplines?" will result in varying opinions from faith bloggers to experts on the subject.

Author Richard Foster has an excellent book entitled, *Celebration of Discipline: The Path to Spiritual Growth*. He categorizes the disciplines as three types: inward, outward, and corporate. Inward habits are meditation, prayer, fasting, and studying the Word. Outward habits are simplicity, solitude, submission, and service. Corporate habits—activities usually associated with church—include confession, worship, guidance, and celebration.

Another book that focuses on the spiritual habits is *Spiritual Disciplines for the Christian Life* by Donald S. Whitney. Whitney expands on the spiritual disciplines that Foster writes about and adds in evangelism, journaling, and learning.

In her book, *Spiritual Disciplines Handbook: Practices That Transforms Us*, Adele Ahlberg Calhoun lists numerous practices that we can engage in to start down the path to spiritual transformation.

In this book, I will be focusing on the spiritual habits that I used to reconnect and draw closer to Jesus. The void of not focusing on Christ left an emptiness in my life. On the outside, my life looked like any normal middle-aged woman, but on the inside, I craved something more, something that only Christ could give me—unconditional love and peace in knowing that whatever trials I face here on earth, eternal life awaits for me in heaven.

However you view the spiritual habits, one thing is clear. As Whitney writes, "Spiritual disciplines are those practices found in Scripture that promote spiritual growth among believers in the gospel of Jesus Christ."[1]

We practice spiritual habits because Christ Himself did. It's that simple. Jesus fasted, prayed, meditated, practiced silence and solitude, and worshiped.

Everyone can practice spiritual habits. The only requirement is a yearning to draw closer to God. You don't need to spend an entire day doing a spiritual habit. However, it does require a daily commitment. How long you spend on your preferred habit is between you and God and no one else.

## For Such a Time as This

Why begin the practice of spiritual habits now? Take a quick look around you, and you will notice that what used to be considered wrong is now slowly blending into the normalcy of life. The difference between black and white is now merged into a gray area. As Christians, we should look different from others, not blend in with the crowd. People should know by looking at us that we are different.

The essential part of practicing spiritual habits is growing in your relationship with Christ and being transformed. We are to be lights of the world (Matthew 5:14) and not conformed to this world (Romans 12:2).

Simply put, we can't be conformed to the world and transformed by Christ at the same time. It's either one or the other—it's never both. And if there has ever been a time to be transformed, it's now.

The book of Esther is one of my favorite books of the Bible. It's filled with twists and turns, ups and downs, and good versus evil. Esther's story contains all the intrigue and scheming that Hollywood blockbusters are made of.

We are introduced to King Ahasuerus, who celebrates his war victories with week-long parties. We meet a strong, dignified queen who refuses to parade herself around the king and his friends in only a crown. Her decision earned her banishment from the palace, thus requiring a new queen to be found. Enter the soon-to-be queen, Esther, and her cousin, Mordecai. Everything seems to be going well until the villain of our blockbuster enters. Haman, King Ahasuerus's right-hand man, shows his true colors. After a falling-out with Mordecai, Haman decides it's best to eliminate the Jewish people. The clueless king falls right into Haman's plot and signs the edict to eradicate God's chosen people.

There is just one problem. The new queen, Esther, is Jewish.

If we were watching this on the big screen, the music would rise to an intense crescendo and the vibrations would flow through our bodies.

Desperate, and rightly so, Mordecai pleads with Queen Esther to approach the king and stop the decree. She reminds her dear cousin that she can't just walk into the room and talk with the king. She needs to be summoned or she could be killed.

Fear overtakes her.

Queen Esther needed a major pep talk, and that's exactly what Mordecai gave her. "Do not think to yourself that in the king's palace you will escape any more than all the other Jews. For if you keep silent at this time, relief and deliverance will rise for the Jews from another place, but you and your father's house will perish. And who knows whether you have not come to the kingdom *for such a time as this?*" (Esther 4:13–14, emphasis mine).

For such a time as this. This phrase is just as relevant to us today as it was to Esther. There is no better time to start practicing spiritual habits.

Now is the time to press pause on social media and pick up our Bibles.

Now is the time to stop comparing ourselves to others and tear down society's expectations of what we need to do, think, and believe.

Now is the time to be spiritually transformed and implement spiritual habits in our lives. We can look toward Queen Esther for guidance.

Yes, it took her a few tries to gather up the courage to tell the king about Haman's plans, but she saved her people from destruction when she did. The same can apply to us. It may take a few tries to get into the routine of practicing the spiritual habits, but the results far outweigh the fear of stepping out in faith and being radically transformed.

## Reigniting the Flame

I wrote this book to share my journey of incorporating spiritual habits in my life. It began with a fateful day in the school parking lot. I will share the good, the bad, and the ugly of my life.

We will begin with a reminder of who we are in Christ and then dive into the spiritual habits. We will study people in the Bible who have been in hills and valleys and have faced many challenges and have come out stronger.

You'll find examples of how to practice spiritual habits and spaces to journal your thoughts. Remember, practicing spiritual habits doesn't mean that your life will automatically be perfect. You will have highs and lows in your life. The trials of living in a broken, sin-filled world may consume you for a season. You will experience spiritual droughts. Do not give up! Refocus back on the One who gave you eternal life. One of the best things about spiritual habits is that they are always there for you to pick back up.

My prayer for you is to understand the spiritual habits better, and most importantly, to begin the journey of spiritual transformation.

Each chapter consists of my personal story, the spiritual habits described in detail, and examples of developing a habit. I include a biblical and personal reflection for you to dig deeper. What you read in the following pages is just the tip of the iceberg. I encourage you to truly dig into the habits and take it upon yourself to research them in greater detail.

Come and join me as we reignite that flame we once had for Christ. The habits we develop will lead us to the one thing we desire most—resting at the feet of Jesus.

# CHAPTER 3

### GIVING IN AND SURRENDERING

*Trust in the LORD with all your heart,*
*and do not lean on your own understanding.*
*In all your ways acknowledge him,*
*and he will make straight your paths.*
Proverbs 3:5–6

"You need to go to this," my husband said.

I glared at him. "I will think about it," I said, expecting that to put an end to the conversation.

My reaction did not deter him. "You are going. End of discussion."

Excuse me? Who did he think he was? Yes, he was my husband, and at our wedding I'd vowed to love, honor, and cherish him, but not obey. Like many couples on their wedding day, we'd omitted the obey part of the traditional wedding vows. As a strong-willed, independent woman, I did not appreciate my husband telling me (not suggesting!) to do something I was not comfortable doing.

Anger boiled up inside of me. Knowing I would say something that I would regret, I spun around and marched into our bedroom. I slammed the door with such force that our wedding photo fell off the wall. Later, with tears in my eyes, I regretted going to that silly church gathering that my in-laws hosted earlier in the evening. I should have trusted my gut instinct and stayed home.

## The Question that Changed My Life

In the days leading up to the gathering, dread and fear overcame me. Even though I had attended my husband's church for a year and a half, I still felt like an outsider. The parishioners were friendly and welcoming, but they were a little too sweet and too "churchy."

My husband, Craig, had grown up in this church, and my in-laws were members before Craig was born. The tiny, close-knit country congregation was more than this city girl could handle. I kept my distance, was cordial to everyone, and spoke when spoken to, but I didn't offer personal information or open up to anyone. So, when my husband told me that his parents were hosting a fall wiener roast for the church on a Sunday evening, I was less than enthused.

In addition to being dragged to the event, I was three and a half months pregnant with our first child. Exhaustion, swollen ankles, and morning sickness plagued me most days. The usual mask of cheerfulness I put on each Sunday morning for an hour and a half would once again have to be put on that evening.

As the evening went on, laughter filled the air and eating commenced. I, admittedly, enjoyed all of it; that is until Jennifer, the minister's wife, approached me with a question. "I'm getting a group of women together to attend a women's conference in Indianapolis, and I was wondering if you would like to join us?" she asked softly.

Immediately, I looked down at my plate and tried desperately to come up with a good excuse not to attend.

Sensing my uncomfortableness, Jennifer continued, "I know that you lived in Indianapolis before you married Craig. I thought this might be a good time to get to know one another, and you can help us get around town."

I gave the classic reply, "Let me check my calendar, and I will get back to you."

In my mind, the answer was a hard no. I was not going away for a weekend with women I barely knew. And as for the conference, it was a two-day Women of Faith conference. There was *no* way that I would be attending an event where women were "holier than thou," thumping their Bibles at me! At that point, I thought many Christians were hypocrites because they thought they were perfect—and no one is perfect. During my childhood, my mother inadvertently taught me that our family of four was considered outcasts to many extended family members who were Christians. In fact, we were raised to believe that those family members were odd and to stay away from them. That's why I didn't even really try to be a Christian; I didn't want to be called strange.

After we returned home from the festivities, the phone rang. I glanced down at the caller ID and mumbled, "So much for waiting on me to call you!" I told my husband to let it go to the answering machine. I had not yet formulated a kind enough response of, "Thank you for asking me, but I'm not going."

This was 2001, and we had an answering machine, not voicemail, so when Jennifer left a message, my husband heard it, loud and clear. And thus, the argument began.

"I think you should go," Craig said.

"No," I replied.

"Honey, you have lived here for over a year and a half. You need to get out and meet others," he said as he held my hands.

"No, I don't! I'm fine!" I lied. He was right. I did want to meet other people and form relationships, but *not* at a Women of Faith conference.

And that's when Craig *told* me I was going to the conference.

Silence surrounded us for the rest of the evening, and he slept on the couch.

## Giving In

In the days following our argument, Craig relentlessly pestered me. Tired of hearing about it and wanting to get him off my back, I gave in and called Jennifer back.

"I'd love to go! Thank you for inviting me!" I lied through my teeth.

A few weeks later, eight of us climbed into two vans and drove three hours east to Indianapolis. Known as the RCA Dome at the time, the arena was packed with women of all ages. Naturally introverted, I was filled with instant regret. I did not belong here. Maybe I could hide? But where? In the bathroom during the whole conference? That was not feasible.

As the light's dimmed, the opening chords of "Shout to the Lord" began. I'd heard the song numerous times in our church services. With little thought to the words, I began to sing along. I didn't realize it at the time, but this was my first experience in participating in a spiritual habit. Worshiping the Lord through music is something that many of us do daily. That Friday night in Indianapolis, the Lord opened my heart and mind as the lyrics to the song enveloped me like a warm blanket on a cold night. Tears welled in my eyes, and I knew my feelings weren't the common pregnancy hormones I had grown accustomed to. A metamorphosis from my old self to a new creation began to take place (2 Corinthians 5:17); however, I was still conflicted. I knew who God was, and I knew who Jesus was and that He died on the cross, but I had no clue about having a personal relationship with Him and what that involved.

As the conference continued, the wall that I had built around my heart and mind slowly came down. Through the tears, laughter, praise, and song, I felt a slight tickle, a fluttering in my stomach area. I'd often felt weird physical sensations since becoming pregnant, but these were different. It wasn't long before I realized that I was feeling my baby, my soon-to-be son, kicking. It was the most fantastic feeling in the world! There, in an arena filled with thousands of women, the Lord chose that moment for me to feel my baby move for the first time. To this day, I tear up thinking about it. That wouldn't be the last time I would see God's hand in that weekend.

## Surrendering All—I'm In!

As we headed back to the hotel, I realized that I had misjudged the women with me. In addition, I realized my bad attitude toward the conference itself had been unfounded. I had definitely been mistaken about what the conference would be like and how I would feel toward it.

The following morning, I woke up with a new sense of purpose. Eager to soak up the speakers' words, I sat in my seat mesmerized. What if the Lord was calling me to be so much more than who I was? What if He wanted me to step out of the life I was living and serve Him? What if I accepted Christ as my Savior? What if I became a Christian?

We came to the point of the conference that I call "check box and accept." If you have ever been to a Christian conference, you know what I am talking about. This is the part of the conference, usually after lunch, where the worship team leads us in some deep worship and prayer. The Holy Spirit is stirring in the arena, and the joy of the Lord is among us.

The speaker announced, "Please take out your conference schedule, and inside you will find a card. If you accepted Christ as your Savior, please check the box that says, 'I'm in!' and provide your contact information."

Without hesitation or a second thought, I checked that box and turned in my card. At the break, I hustled down to the conference shop and bought my first Bible. Holding it proudly in my hands, I turned from the table and spotted Jennifer.

"What did you buy?" she asked innocently.

"A Bible," I replied.

"You don't own a Bible?"

"No, but I just gave my life to Christ, so I figured I better get one so I can learn more about Him."

With a look of happiness and a little shock, Jennifer embraced me and said, "Congratulations!"

As we made our way back to our seats, I couldn't contain my joy! I held in my hands a book, *the* book—the *Women of Faith NIV Study Bible* paperback edition with purple font— it was mine. It was new and crisp. As I scanned through the pages, my emotions overtook me—this book contained words that I longed for.

Something had been missing in my life, but I didn't know what until that moment. It's hard to describe, but the feeling that came over me was one of peace and calmness. A heaviness lifted, and I knew that from that moment on, my life would never be the same. I never realized how lost I was until I found Christ in the former RCA Dome in Indianapolis, Indiana.

Can you relate to this feeling? If you accepted Christ as your Lord and Savior, your spiritual transformation began the minute you said yes. You felt the change in your heart and soul. You viewed your life and others around you differently. Christ was working in you and through you. If you haven't accepted Christ as your Savior, I encourage you to take some time and sit quietly with the Lord. Prayerfully, lay out your concerns before Him and seek to find the One who loves you unconditionally.

# CHAPTER 4

## A NEW OUTLOOK

*For God so loved the world,*
*that he gave his only Son,*
*that whoever believes in him*
*should not perish but have eternal life.*
John 3:16

The Missy that walked out the door Friday afternoon, growling and grumbling about attending a Christian women's conference, returned utterly different. The moment I walked into our home, my husband saw the change.

"It was incredible!" I said. "The speakers' messages, the laughter, and the music. I made a lot of new friends, and I accepted Christ as my Savior."

Craig hugged me. For the first time since moving to Illinois, I felt accepted, and I found a group of women who would be by my side through some of my darkest days. I also apologized to my husband. He knew what was best for me. He wanted me to establish lifelong friendships, but more importantly, he wanted me to meet the Savior. Craig wanted nothing more than his wife to accept Christ as her Savior so together we could raise our son in a godly, Christian home.

Eager to get to church the following morning, I entered the building doors with a fresh perspective on Christ and my faith. My heart raced as I clutched my new Bible and hung on every word the minister said. Like a sponge, soaking in everything within reach, my heart and mind reached out to gain a better understanding of God. That understanding would only come from reading and studying the Bible.

But as a new believer, where did I begin? Did I start at the beginning with Genesis? Or with the Psalms? Or should I skip right to the end to Revelation?

A week after the life-changing conference, my friend Barbara asked me to have lunch with her. Still thirsty to know everything about Jesus, I began to tell her about both the excitement and the frustration I felt. How can I quench this thirst? Where do I even start, and more importantly, how can I understand it?

"Start reading the book of John," Barbara said. "The Gospel of John reflects on the life of Christ, and you will gain a better understanding of Him," she explained. That was exactly what I needed—a better understanding of who Christ is and how I have eternal life through His death and resurrection.

After our girl's day out, I returned home, intending to know Jesus on a more personal level. Grabbing my Bible, I sat down in the most comfortable chair that could accommodate my pregnant body and began this new relationship.

With a deep breath and high hopes, I dug into the first verse. "In the beginning was the Word, and the Word was with God, and the Word was God" (John 1:1).

Huh?

What did that verse mean? What beginning? Who is the Word? My questions outweighed my desire to learn more. My quest for spiritual water ran into a dried-up well with no hope of replenishment. The only moisture came from the tears streaming down my face—the anticipation of what I once eagerly longed for extinguished. You can call it failure to comprehend or even "pregnancy fog."

Both would be a fair assessment. I felt inadequate and underqualified to continue.

Deflated, I closed my Bible.

*Is this how it's going to be, Lord? I yearn to know you more, but how can I when I don't understand even the very first verse of John?* Looking back to this moment that occurred over nineteen years ago, I realize now it was the enemy at work. He was not happy with the spiritual transformation happening in my life and decided to throw more fear, doubt, frustration, and anxiety at me. Working overtime, he continued to try to derail me hoping I would give up and retreat to my old lifestyle. Thankfully, the Lord was holding me tightly and lighting the path to His Word.

In times of trouble and despair, or during our feeble attempts to understand the Word better, He gives us the equipment. God's Word is a lamp to guide us when the enemy is working against us (Psalm 119:105).

The next day, I returned to the Gospel of John. This time a wave of peace fell over me. I was beginning to incorporate a spiritual habit, and I didn't even realize it. That's what is so amazing about these habits. When we read our Bibles, say our prayers, or commit Scripture to memory, we are practicing a spiritual habit. We just never put a name to it.

Four months after checking the "I'm in" box, I took the next step in growing my faith by publicly declaring my new life in Christ. The joy and happiness of that decision came at a cost, and I would soon know what it would be like to live the words that Jesus spoke over his disciples, "If the world hates you, know that it has hated me before it hated you," (John 15:18).

## Immersed and Made New

As I stepped into the warm, inviting water from within the open-windowed baptistry, I looked out to see my small church congregation looking intently toward me and the baptistry. I thought about what led to this moment, and it felt like I was dreaming. Or maybe

I was living in a Hallmark movie? A big-city girl in a small country church ready to give her life to the One who never left her side. How did I get here?

While the Women of Faith conference sparked the fire of my radical transformation, it was the forgiveness and the love of Christ and my surrendering and trusting in Him that brought me to the baptistry. With tears of happiness and joy, followed by many prayers, it was time to stop living life on my own. With a feeling of relief and inclusion, my new church family embraced me from the moment I stepped into the church. A church fellowship that I once resisted now supported me with love and joy. After the Women of Faith conference, this caring church community never left our side when Craig's oldest son unexpectedly passed away. They stayed with me when I went into premature labor. As I glanced at the sanctuary, smiles greeted me. And for the first time, I knew that I belonged and that I was loved.

Happily married and with a baby on the way, my life probably looked perfect to many people. But on the inside, I knew something had been missing.

After twenty-nine years of trying to do life on my own, I finally gave in to the desire to be wanted and loved unconditionally. I gave up trying to live life on my own. Yes, my husband was loving and supportive, but I lacked something more significant than what Craig could provide.

Growing up, I viewed the Lord as an authoritative, judgmental figure who would constantly remind me of my failures—much like my mom did. I believed that Jesus was the Son of God, but that was the extent of it. While growing up, we celebrated Christmas and Easter, but focused on the secular side. We were a mixed religion family—my mother was Catholic, and my father was Mennonite. I did not have the advantage of participating in Bible studies or small groups. I longed to belong somewhere, anywhere, to escape the friction of my home life. Unfortunately, instead of turning to the One who would save me, I turned to unhealthy vices and relationships.

That day in the baptistry, a revolutionary thought occurred to me: After years of longing for a genuine relationship and desperately wanting to belong somewhere, I discovered that I myself was the cause of my discontentment.

I realized that a veil of self-centeredness and control stood between the Lord and me. That veil needed to be removed for me to see the love of God. I did belong to and always had belonged to Someone. After my spiritual blindness lifted, I realized that my sense of belonging to someone had been with me since the Lord knitted me in my mother's womb (Psalm 139:13). I just needed to release the chains that bound my heart and grasp onto the Lord's outstretched hand that had been waiting for me to become a believer.

Once that veil was lifted, I was ready to publicly admit that I was a sinner, that I believed Jesus was the Son of God, that He died on the cross for my sins, and on the third day rose from the grave. I would be immersed in water and confess my faith in Jesus as Lord of my life. These three things—admit, believe, confess—are the ABCs of becoming a Christian.

After I publicly proclaimed these essentials, the minister gently tipped me back and immersed me in the warm water. The rushing waters took away the emptiness that I had felt for many years and replaced it with the love of a Savior who never has and never will leave or forsake me.

As I came up out of that water, my old self was gone, and a new creation was born. I was living out Paul's words in 2 Corinthians 5:17, "Therefore, if anyone is in Christ, he is a new creation. The old has passed away; behold, the new has come."

My life was instantly made new in Christ. In celebration, the creation that the Lord had entrusted me to raise into a godly man, enthusiastically kicked inside my womb. With tears of joy for both the new life growing inside me and my new life in Christ, I was finally at a place where happiness overcame my sadness.

I was living out Galatians 3:26–28, which reads, "For in Christ Jesus you are all sons of God, through faith. For as many of you as were baptized into Christ have put on Christ. There is neither Jew nor Greek, there is neither slave nor free, there is no male and female, for you are all one in Christ Jesus."

I was one in Christ Jesus.

Yes, life was finally the way I always envisioned it. I belonged and was loved—both by my heavenly Father and by my husband.

However, while my spiritual life grew, another relationship started to unravel. My bond with my mom, already frayed for my moving out-of-state after getting married, disintegrated further. Mom was none too happy with my new life.

I called my parents, excited about my new life in Christ, only to face criticism.

"Why? We baptized you as an infant," Mom questioned.

As I explained my reasoning, her response stung me to the core.

"Do you think you are better than us now that you go to church?"

Ouch. In her eyes, I am now one of *those* people who considered themselves better than others.

I'd heard of Christian persecution in other parts of the world but never thought I'd experience it in my own family. My mom believed that I thought I was better than her because I was a practicing Christian. No matter how hard I tried to convince her that I wasn't perfect and that I was still a sinner, and that I still messed up in areas of my daily life, her animosity toward me grew stronger each year and was still in full effect until the day she died.

Torn between living my life for Christ or trying to appease my mom, I realized that I needed to do what was best for me, my husband, and our soon-to-be family.

The day I was baptized was the beginning of the end of my relationship with my mom. I chose Jesus over my mom, and she never forgave me for it.

## Two Steps Forward, Three Steps Back

As my relationship with Christ grew, I knew for certain who Jesus was. Through His Word, I encountered a Savior who humbly stepped off His heavenly throne and took the form of a man. Born of a virgin, this man came into the world to save us from our sins and give us eternal life through His death and resurrection. I soaked up every word, and if I didn't understand what I read, I called Barbara, and she was able to walk me through things and explain them to me.

Four weeks after baptism, one of the two greatest joys in my life occurred: the birth of our son, Grant. As a new believer on fire for the Lord, I was determined to continue to fan the flame that was ignited in me that precious day I was baptized. After all, how hard could it be to stay on fire for the Lord and raise children?

The short answer is it was a lot harder than I ever could have imagined!

## Coming Full Circle

After the birth of my children, Grant and Connor, I was in full mom mode and going through the motions as a believer. My flame for the Lord turned into a list of to-dos that I would check off weekly.

√ Go to church every Sunday—check!
√ Sign up for Bible study—check!
√ Quickly fill in the blanks of said Bible study, so I didn't look like a slacker in front of the other moms—check!

The list could go on.

I had the most important job in the world, but I'd lost my identity. It wasn't my children's fault that I slipped into lukewarm faith. Instead, I took on the identity of mom and poured everything I had into that identity. I put my children before the Lord and my husband.

Something needed to change.

I needed a radical transformation, and I needed that fire reignited. This change needed to happen not only for myself but for my children as well. They needed a mom who was refreshed, recharged, and rejuvenated. They needed a mom who, at the beginning of the day, hit the floor on her knees in prayer instead of checking Facebook.

Perhaps you are like me. You need to be reminded of your identity. You need to reignite that flame. You need to come full circle.

To do this, we will need to step outside our comfort zone, make sacrifices, and say no to things that do not align with the Lord's will for our life.

Spiritual transformation begins from within and works its way outward. As the Lord changes us from the inside, our outward appearance can change. Of course, this doesn't mean that lines and wrinkles will magically go away (oh, how I wish!) but that others will see a change that reflects the Lord's work in us.

## Spirit Not of Fear

Please do not let fear stop you from fulfilling the life that God wants you to lead! In 2 Timothy 1:7, the Lord reminds us that He gave us a "spirit not of fear but power and love and self-control." This verse came to me while I was walking a labyrinth at my local retreat center. As I was wrestling with the decision to step out in faith and trust the Lord, I felt the Spirit whisper this verse to me—one that I had read numerous times before. Repeating the phrase "spirit not of fear" over and over, I realized that the Lord had fully equipped me to do what He was calling me to do. I just needed to step over the wall of fear and follow Him.

Have you ever encountered something like this? Have you sensed the Lord wants you to step out in faith to start living for Him? The Lord is telling you that everything is under His control.

It's time to come full circle and live the life that the Lord has intended for you to live. It's time to drink from the well of living water.

# CHAPTER 5

## BIBLICAL REFLECTION— AN INVITATION TO DRINK FROM THE WELL OF LIVING WATER

*But whoever drinks of the water that I will give him*
*will never be thirsty again.*
*The water that I will give him will become in him*
*a spring of water welling up to eternal life.*
John 4:14

*I* love the story of the Samaritan woman at the well in John 4. Despite her life being a chaotic mess and an embarrassment, Jesus chose her to spread the news that He was the Messiah, the One who Isaiah, Jeremiah, Hosea, and other prophets spoke of. The prophecy from the Old Testament had been fulfilled.

If Jesus picked a woman who was culturally rejected to spread the Good News about Him, imagine what He can do for you! You may be tired, burned out, and feeling inadequate, but He is not done with you. No matter what you have done in your past or the present, your Savior will use you to further His kingdom.

Let's dig into this story a little deeper.

The Samaritans were from, you guessed it, the city of Samaria in the Northern Kingdom of Israel. In 722 BC, the city was conquered by the Assyrians, and about 27,000 Israelites were deported to Assyria. Those who were deported were high class and skilled workers. Some of the remaining Samaritans married Gentiles that the Assyrians brought in from other lands to repopulate Israel. When the Israelites returned to the land, the rift of racial and religious tensions grew between the Samaritans and the Jews. The Jews treated the Samaritans with contempt; thus, the Jewish people avoided the Samaritans at all costs. However, the Samaritans worshiped the same God as the Jews did. The same God that was their God forever reigns as our God.

Studying from the first five books of the Bible (Genesis through Deuteronomy), the Samaritans held on to hope of Moses or someone like him returning one day to save them.

The Samaritan woman looked for a savior to relieve her of the pain and humiliation she faced daily. Little did she know that by gathering water in the midday sun, her life would be impacted, and Jesus would use her to spread the gospel.

If there were ever a mic drop in the Bible, it would be this. In those days, a Jewish man would not be caught in public speaking to a (1) woman, (2) a Samaritan, or (3) an adulteress.

But Jesus wasn't an ordinary Jewish man, was He?

She chose the noon hour on purpose because no one would be at the well in the heat of the day. No one would be there to whisper behind her back, to judge her. She was the talk of the town, damaged goods. She was tired, hurt, and just wanted to be loved. Physically, she was thirsty; however, she would learn quickly that she was also spiritually thirsty.

Jesus was exhausted from His long journey with His disciples. They were heading back to Galilee, and while most Jews skirted around Samaria, Jesus and his disciples traveled right through it. His reason for stopping at the well wasn't only to get a drink—it was to meet her.

As she approached Jacob's well, she saw Him. Jews did not associate with her kind, so why was He there at *that* moment? What did He want? He knew all about her life. What she had hidden in the darkness would soon be brought into the light. He knew what she desperately wanted, what she needed—a life. And not just *any* life, but *eternal life.*

Known in her town as a nobody, the Samaritan woman went through husbands as quickly as I go through the Chick-fil-A drive-through for a sweet tea. Never satisfied, hoping for love and security, she moved on to the next man, only to be met with the same disappointing results. After being married five times, the man she was living with was far from being a husband. Her promiscuous lifestyle was wearing on her. She had given up hope, was just going through the motions and trying to get by. She was of ill-repute and morally despised by her people. She just wanted to go to the well for water and do so in peace.

Enter Jesus the Messiah, the Savior of the world, who would change all our lives. The apostle John states in John 4:6 that Jesus was worn out from His journey, showing that He was indeed human. We all know how it feels to be worn out and weary from traveling, especially if we travel with our children. Think about it. He was traveling with His disciples, and I'm sure on more than one occasion they asked, "Are we there yet?"

Jesus spoke first. "Give me a drink."

Imagine her surprise when Jesus initiated their conversation, completely breaking the cultural barrier. Her response bordered on sarcastic. "How is it that you, *a Jew*, ask for a drink from me, a woman from Samaria?" (John 4:9, emphasis mine).

She expected hostility. Jesus responded with care and compassion. "If you knew the gift of God, and who it is that is saying to you, 'Give me a drink,' you would have asked him, and he would have given you living water" (John 4:10).

Intrigued, she asked, "Where do you get living water?" He had no way to draw water from the well. *Who is this man?* She believed Him to be a prophet, and she would see soon enough that He was more significant than she could have ever imagined.

"Everyone who drinks of this water will be thirsty again, but whoever drinks of the water that I will give him will never be thirsty again" (John 4:13–14).

And just like that, Jesus let her know that He was her Savior. Her Refuge. Her Strength. Her Eternal Life. Her Living Water. She wanted what He was offering. Jesus had one last request of her: "Go, call your husband, and come here."

"I have no husband," she replied.

"You are right in saying, 'I have no husband,' for you have had five husbands, and the one you now have is not your husband. What you have said is true" (John 9:17–18, author's paraphrase).

I can only imagine that she was in complete awe at this time. He knew about her life, the darkness she lived in, and He still spoke to her.

Who does that?

Jesus, the Son of God, that's who.

Her final statement to Him was, "I know that Messiah is coming (he who is called Christ). When he comes, he will tell us all things."

Jesus said to her, "I who speak to you, am he" (John 4:25–26).

Simple and to the point, but so impactful for all to hear.

## Life after Meeting Jesus

The Samaritan woman left her water jar at the well and went straight into town to tell the people that the Messiah was there. She threw off the guilt, shame, hurt, and darkness that had been plaguing her for so many years. She now had all that she needed, all that she ever needed. Living water. Eternal life.

Because of her testimony, many Samaritans became believers. And Jesus didn't just pass on through Samaria. He stayed for two days talking with them about the Living Water that He was to them.

Jesus invites us to take the cup from Him and never be thirsty. What's holding you back from taking that cup? Pride? Shamefulness? Whatever it is, He already knows all about your life, and guess what? He still loves you! Jesus knows everything about us, so let's take some time to get to know more about Him through practicing spiritual habits.

## Reflection and Journal Questions

1. If you can remember your baptism day, reflect on being a new believer. If you were baptized as an infant, what does it mean to you now? Journal your thoughts. How did you feel? What emotions did you have?

2. Meditate on 2 Timothy 1:7. What is the Lord equipping you to do but you are afraid to step out in faith and do? Journal your answer and hand over your fears to Him.

3. Read the account of the Samaritan woman in John 4:1–30. Did you discover something new reading it? What stood out to you?

4. Do you have any doubts that Jesus doesn't love you because of your past sins? Cast those thoughts out and write a letter to Jesus thanking Him for His unconditional love for you.

# *PART 2*

## YOUR IDENTITY IS IN CHRIST, NOT THE WORLD

*But to all who did receive him,*
*who believed in his name,*
*he gave the right*
*to become children of God.*
John 1:12

# CHAPTER 6

## Mayhem in the Middle School Parking Lot

*And we know that for those who love God*
*all things work together for good,*
*for those who are called according to his purpose.*
Romans 8:28

Before we dive into the spiritual habits that will lead us on the path of spiritual transformation, we need to remember who we are in Christ. Our identities in Christ are essential to knowing that Christ sees us differently than the world sees us.

Our worldly identities are based on what others see, such as our economic status and accomplishments. It's easy for us to get caught up in those identities and strive for perfection as a wife, mom, career woman, volunteer, and so on.

Our lives on social media play a big part in our worldly identities too. Most of my posts are about the good things in my life, such as significant life moments, photos of our family vacations, and the perfect family photo. If I were a betting woman, I would wager that your social media posts are along the same line as mine.

What we don't post is our personal and family struggles. A woman could be dealing with depression and grief. A child may be dealing with substance abuse or pornography addiction. The family vacation may be a last-ditch effort to save a marriage. And that perfect family photo? A colossal argument occurred right before the camera clicked, and the smiles on our faces are as fake as Monopoly money.

Life is hard.

Life is painful.

Life is troublesome.

Thankfully, we have a Savior who has come to give us hope. In the various translations of the Bible, not one time does it say that believer's lives will be perfect or that we will escape trouble or be happy all the days of our lives.

The Bible tells us the opposite. In the Gospel of John, Jesus confirmed that we *would* have trouble. "I have told you all this so that you may have peace in me. Here on earth you will have many trials and sorrows. But take heart, because I have overcome the world" (John 16:33 NLT).

Such wise words from the Savior of the world!

But even as we face troubles and trials, our identity does not change. It is secure in Christ, no matter what we do or don't accomplish.

In this chapter we will reflect on our identities in Christ and how spiritual habits keep us focused on our true identities.

But first, I want to share that life-changing day in the middle school parking lot. It wasn't my finest moment as a parent, but it was a moment the Lord orchestrated to wake me up and show me that the life I was living wasn't the one He wanted me to live.

## Unacceptable

"What in the world is taking those boys so long?" I grumbled to myself.

Every day at 3:30 p.m., I repeated the same question. Day after day, it was the same mundane routine; waiting, sighing, and scanning

Facebook on my phone while I waited for my children in the school parking lot. My boys were notorious for taking their time leaving the building. The longer I waited, the more frustrated I became. I didn't have a moment to spare. I was busy. Too busy. Didn't my children realize that? They may not have recognized the busy mom, but they knew all too well the mom that could snap at them at a moment's notice.

I was tired and cranky. Overwhelmed and stressed. Caught up in the "Yes, I can do that!" life. I did it all.

"Can you collect supplies for the auction?"

"Yes, I can do that!"

"Would you mind organizing the room party?"

"Sure can!"

"I know you are busy, but we need an extra hand to_____ (fill in the blank)."

"No problem at all!"

I was a people pleaser. I didn't want to say no to anyone who asked for my help. That's what Christians are supposed to do, right? Always say yes to helping others? While I continued my pattern of never saying no, the Holy Spirit started to work on my heart. Slowly, He began to show me that my people pleasing was an idol and needed to be demolished immediately. The more I said yes to others, the more I pushed the Lord away. I promised the Lord that someday I would put Him first in my life, but until then I felt my calling was to help others. This revealed that living to please people and living to please the Lord do not always go hand in hand. Usually, it's one or the other, and while I felt the pressing of the Spirit to reignite that fire that had burned after my baptism, I couldn't let go of the grip of the human approval I found in pleasing others.

So, I continued to say yes to everyone—except Christ. Lukewarm in my faith and going through the motions, my time with Christ was more of a checkmark. I participated in Bible studies and volunteered at church, but my heart was not into it. Twelve years ago, I had been on fire for Christ, but now the fire was replaced by embers, the flame extinguished. I was going through the motions, wandering through the wilderness, and losing my identity in Christ along the way.

*Where is the fire and passion I once had?* I sighed again.

Glancing around the school parking lot, I noticed that all the moms looked the same: tired and worn out. As our children entered the middle school years, sports and after-school activities increased. Many were held in different locations, so we often sped out of the parking lot, hurrying to get our children to their next practice on time.

This particular day I needed to get my youngest son, Connor, to the soccer field across town. Pressed for time, short on patience, and growing frustrated by the minute, I gripped the steering wheel, locked my arms straight out, and leaned my head back on the seat rest. *Is this what I've been reduced to? A mom taxi driver?*

Finally, I saw Grant exiting the school doors, smiling and chatting with his friends. *Seriously? He's had all day to talk with his friends; we've got to get going!* In one fluid motion, I grabbed the car door handle, flung my seatbelt off, and met Grant in the middle of the parking lot.

"Where is your brother?" I growled.

The smile faded from his face. "I don't know."

"What do you mean you don't know? He's got practice. Go back in and find him!"

Grant's once bright smile was gone, replaced by a stunned look. His mom had taken the wind out of his sail. Shoulders slumped, Grant turned around and headed back toward the school doors. For a split second, I felt like the worst mom in the world. My son, excited to see me, was yelled at by his stressed out, overcommitted mom in the middle school parking lot. Grant was almost to the school entrance when Connor finally appeared. Sauntering side by side, both my sons appeared utterly oblivious to my urgency to get Connor to practice on time.

"Get in the van *now!*" I screamed. The remorse I'd felt had dissipated.

Moving a tad quicker, they hopped in the back seat and buckled up. I unleashed my pent-up anger.

"You knew that we were in a hurry today, and you both took your time getting out of school! This is not acceptable, and if you can't get out here quicker than this, Connor, I'm pulling you out of soccer. This is ridiculous!" The sheer look of hurt on his face after my rant is still ingrained in my mind today.

"Mr. Smith needed some help cleaning up his classroom after our Bible project today," Connor quietly said, "so I stayed after to help him."

Chastened, I drove in silence for the rest of the way. Both boys have a heart for servanthood, and Connor's love language is acts of service. He volunteered to stay after school to help despite knowing that he might be late for practice.

This was my wake-up call. Not only were my actions that day unacceptable, but my children also saw a side of me that reminded me of some of the qualities I had not liked about my own mother. I needed a change in life and attitude. I needed to become the best mom I could be, and more importantly, I needed to place Christ first in my life.

## Grab Your Bible Instead

The next day, like clockwork, I was back in the middle school pick-up line, but this time my wait was different. For years, I carried a small, compact Bible in my purse, intending to read it during downtimes, such as waiting for my children to exit the school building. Instead, it had become another object that I transferred from purse to purse.

But this time, as I reached for my phone, I felt the Holy Spirit nudge me to grab my Bible instead. Sifting through my purse, I felt the Good Book at the very bottom, and I grabbed it. The cover was worn and torn, not due to use but to the numerous things thrown on it. The pages, however, were intact and crisp—barely used.

I glanced at the clock and noted I had about five minutes until the boys would come out. That was enough time to take in a verse or two. I went straight to John 3:16, the most well-known verse in the Bible and one that I had read many times before: "For God so loved the world, that he gave his only Son, that whoever believes in him should not perish but have eternal life."

What followed is hard to explain. Those five minutes of studying Scripture changed my attitude, reminded me of my true identity, and gave me a fresh start on my path of spiritual transformation. From that day forward, I used my time in the pickup line to study Scripture and to answer a few questions from the Bible study I was currently working on. As time went on, the Lord revealed my identities in Christ. Yes, I am a mom, but I am also a daughter of the King, and through Christ, I am so much more.

By finding my identity in Christ, I become a better mother. Waiting in the pickup line wasn't so bad after all.

# CHAPTER 7

## EMBRACING YOUR IDENTITY IN CHRIST

*I have been crucified with Christ.*
*It is no longer I who live, but Christ who lives in me.*
*And the life I now live in the flesh I live by faith*
*in the Son of God, who loved me and gave himself for me.*
Galatians 2:20

Maybe like me, you have struggled to remember who you are in Christ, and you have lost your identity. You yearn to be the woman that the Lord says you are, but you are trying to meet the world's Pinterest perfect expectations.

Or maybe you are overcommitted and losing sight of the Lord's purpose and will for your life. For me, overcommitment led to late nights, early mornings, unhealthy eating habits, and low energy. Frequent yelling and impatience resulted. While Bible study friends and those I served with saw the people pleasing, smiling Missy, my husband and children saw the "can be set off by anything that we do wrong" Missy.

I longed to find purpose beyond the everydayness of my roles but didn't know where to begin. I began to pray, asking God to show me how to restore my passion for Him.

As I share the steps I took that led me back to Christ, and I invite you to use them as examples as you try to do the same.

First, set aside the expectations the world has for you and turn to the One who knows you better than you know yourself. Jesus Christ, our Savior, is the glue that holds our lives together. Putting Christ first in our lives reveals our true identities. By focusing less on how the world sees us, and more on how Christ sees us, our *true* identity will become more visible.

We will learn how to find our identities, not in our roles or circumstances, but in God's definition of who we are.

While we will find other truths of who we are in Scripture, these are the keystones. Grab your Bible, and let's dig into Scripture to discover more about these truths.

## Who We Are in Christ

A quick Google search of "Who I am in Christ?" brings up pages upon pages of websites with one main goal, to remind us of the numerous Bible verses of God's love for us.

On the days when life gets the best of us, we can feel down and out, unloved, and uncared for. This is when we need to lean on our Savior. In spite of the many verses that remind us of our true identities in Christ, our enemy will counterattack and confront us with how the world views us. By equipping ourselves with the Word and practicing the spiritual habits, we can defend ourselves when the enemy attacks. Never forget that the oppressor is constantly on the move. "Be sober-minded; be watchful. Your adversary the devil prowls around like a roaring lion, seeking someone to devour" (1 Peter 5:8).

The enemy isn't idle. He doesn't sit around waiting for us to sin. He's on the move, prowling around like a lion stalking his next lunch. We've all seen the videos in which a sweet gazelle is oblivious to the lurking danger in the high weeds. She's focused on what is in front of her. By the time the gazelle realizes her enemy is watching her, it's too late. But it's not too late for us. Yes, we will sin, and yes, the enemy pounces, but through Christ, we have forgiveness. We still have eternal life. The enemy has eternal hell.

In Christ, we are:

- Adopted as God's Child (Ephesians 1:5)
- Alive (Romans 6:11)
- Anointed with the Holy Spirit (1 John 2:27)
- A temple (1 Corinthians 3:17)
- Beloved (Romans 1:7)
- Chosen (Ephesians 1:4–6)
- Crucified with Christ (Galatians 2:20)
- God's workmanship (Ephesians 2:10)
- Filled with the fruit of the Spirit (Galatians 5:22)
- Free (John 8:36)
- Forgiven (Colossians 1:14)
- Justified by faith (Romans 5:1)
- Loved (Galatians 2:20)
- Protected from the enemy (John 17:15)
- New creation (2 Corinthians 5:17)
- No longer a slave to sin (Romans 6:6)
- Redeemed by the shed blood of Christ (Ephesians 1:7)
- Seated with Christ (Ephesians 2:6)
- Salt of the earth and light of the earth (Matthew 5:13–14)

These are just a handful of our identities in Christ. Amid the chaos of the world we stand on the solid rock of Christ. Let's embrace our identities and never forget that we are His and His alone. We don't belong to the government, and we don't even belong to our husbands or families. We belong to God.

## My Identity Is in Christ Alone

My mom and I had a close relationship while I lived at home. I will be the first one to admit that the angst of my teenage years strained the bonds we'd enjoyed in my childhood. The tighter she tried to control me, the more I rebelled.

After those rebellious, tear-stained years, I realized that through it all, my mom was the only consistent, stable person in my life. Throughout my college years, I looked forward to her phone calls, letters, and our mother-daughter trips.

Things remained relatively unchanged after my college graduation. When I became engaged to my husband, my mom and I planned my wedding together. From designing the flowers to trips to Hobby Lobby to buy the reception decor, to choosing the colors, we did it side by side.

We went to the bridal shops in search of the perfect dress, only to be disappointed with the results. None of them screamed, "Say yes to the dress!"

After scouring the bridal magazines, I finally found the dress of my dreams.

"That is similar to my wedding dress. You could wear mine!" my mom said with enthusiasm.

I hesitated. My parents were married in 1969. Having viewed their wedding album throughout the years, I knew styles had changed considerably in thirty years. Hello, big hair and bright, psychedelic colors!

To appease her, I agreed to help her get the dress down from the attic and at least look at it. As we examined it, I realized my mom was right. Her gown did look similar to the dress I had found in the magazine. So, with some alternations—removing the sleeves and letting out the waist—I had found the perfect wedding dress.

Our relationship continued strong, even though we lived in different states; however, on the afternoon of my baptism, everything changed.

As my relationship with Christ grew, my relationship with my mom deteriorated. She couldn't stomach the fact that we were raising our children in a Protestant, not a Catholic, church. Although my family hadn't participated in a mass for over fifteen years, my mom still considered us all to be Catholics, even though my husband was not.

Tipping the scales of our relationship was the fact that we sent our children to a Christian school. "Is a public school not good enough for the boys?" my mom sneered when I told her we would be moving the boys from a public to a private school.

Adding fuel to the fire was the fact that my mom was a lifelong alcoholic. Throughout the years, her drinking intensified to the point where she would become belligerent and verbally abusive. One of my childhood chores was to have a drink ready for her when she got home from work. Back then, I was an obedient child; however, I now realize I was fueling my mom's alcohol addiction.

Still, determined to have a relationship with her and to keep her involved in her grandsons' lives, I called her weekly. I made it a point to either call her at work or fifteen minutes after she got home. Any later than that, she would be drunk.

Due to our "lifestyle," my parents refused to visit us, so we always traveled to them. In the few days leading up to our visits, my anxiety level would be through the roof. How would I be treated this time? Would it be better than the previous visits? Like a scene from the movie, *Groundhog Day*, each visit started the same. From the moment we walked into the house, my mom would greet Craig and the boys with hugs, and completely ignore me. She was already drunk, slurring her words and using every means possible to put me down. Due to the toxic environment, we didn't stay at their house but in a hotel. I would often go back to the room in tears, pleading with Craig to drive us back home. Emotionally and physically drained from her verbal abuse, my spirit was crushed beyond repair.

The following morning, she would be a normal mom and grandma, happy to see us and loving on us. It would always be short-lived, as she consumed alcohol throughout the day, becoming the woman I had grown accustomed to.

Our last visit changed our relationship forever, with no opportunity to reconcile. Four months later, her death ended all her pain and suffering, and subsequently, closed the door on the reconciliation that I longed for.

During that visit, while I was holding my youngest son, my mom physically attacked me. Angry over something I supposedly said at my grandfather's funeral months before, her brewing resentment came to a head, and she grabbed my arm, spewing, "I hate you! You are nothing to me!"

I jerked my arm away from her grip and shielded my son from his grandma. I exploded with a slew of words that I wished I could take back—among them being that she would never see her grandchildren again.

My dad tried to defuse the situation by making excuses for my mom's behavior. It was too late. There would be no more excuses. With a broken heart and eyes stained with tears, we went back to the hotel.

My mom's words were gut-wrenching.

I was nothing to her.

The Lord, however, reminded me that I was everything to Him. He reminded me that identity is in Christ and Christ alone.

## Living a Life Guided by the Holy Spirit

Although our identity in Christ is secure, we are not immune to the desires of the flesh. In Galatians 5:16, Paul states by walking in the Spirit, we will "not gratify the desires of the flesh." We can conquer our fleshly desires by being led and guided by the Holy Spirit and yielding to His power. Those fleshly desires tend to overtake us when "the spirit indeed is willing, but the flesh is weak" (Matthew 26:41).

What exactly are those fleshly desires, you may ask? Paul has graciously listed them all for us in Galatians 5:19–21. They include sexual immorality, impurity, idolatry, strife, jealousy, fits of anger, rivalries, dissensions, divisions, envy, drunkenness, and "things like these." It sounds like a day on social media!

In a world filled with fleshly desires, we know we shouldn't do them, but they are so satisfying that we give in to them. Once we serve our needs, we regret engaging in desires such as food, drugs and alcohol, pornography, control, envy, or excess spending. We confess our sins and promise never to do it again—until the desire comes back. It's a never-ending cycle.

Thankfully, the Lord sends the Holy Spirit to indwell us and plant the seeds needed to have a fruitful life.

# CHAPTER 8

## FRUIT OF THE SPIRIT

*But the fruit of the Spirit is love*
*joy, peace, kindness, goodness,*
*faithfulness, gentleness, self-control;*
*against such things there is no law.*
Galatians 5:22–23

Raise your hand if you have always read Galatians 5:22–23 as "fruits" of the Spirit, instead of "fruit" of the Spirit? I did, and at times, still do today. In elementary school, we learned that if we see a list with multiple items, we needed to add an *s* to the end of the subject. In this case, the fruit of the Spirit is viewed as one unit. "But the fruit of the Spirit is love, joy, peace, kindness, goodness, faithfulness, gentleness, self-control; against such things there is no law" (Galatians 5:22–23).

The apostle Paul uses the term *fruit* for these Godly characteristics as representing unity and a living product of the Holy Spirit. We do not produce these characteristics on our own, and it's only through the Holy Spirit that we obtain them. Only those who proclaim Jesus as their Lord and Savior and live by faith possess these characteristics. If you accepted Jesus as your Savior, you have the fruit of the Spirit. But like the process of spiritual transformation, our fruit or characteristics of the Spirit develop and grow over time—a lot of time.

My husband is the gardener of the family, and every year before Christmas he starts planning the garden. He meticulously designs the layout of where each plant will go and when they need to be planted. He then begins ordering from his favorite seed company. Between our Christmas gifts and regular mail deliveries, we receive small packages of tiny seeds for broccoli, cabbage, cauliflower, peppers, and tomatoes.

As the weather turns warmer, Craig begins the process of growing these seeds into plants. He fills the containers with fertilized soil, plants the tiny seeds, and places them under growing lamps. With the daily tasks of watering, adjusting the lights, and more fertilizer, those seeds—the size of the tip of a needle—begin to sprout through the soil.

Once they start to grow, Craig doesn't stop caring for them. They still need water and light. When spring comes and the weather turns warmer, Craig transfers all the plants into the garden. Throughout the spring and summer months, they continue to grow, but they still need help to produce the desired fruit or vegetable. Craig cultivates the soil and waters the plants until they are harvested. We enjoy the fruits of his labor as we feast on the fresh tomatoes, green beans, lettuce, potatoes, and cucumbers. Abundant yields mean extra harvest—sometimes enough to give away to friends and family in addition to our own freezing and canning. Our garden continues to provide during the winter months with homemade tomato juices, spaghetti sauce, and salsa.

Craig continues to cultivate and care for the plants after they're planted, in the same way the Holy Spirit works in us producing the fruit of the Spirit. We do not and cannot produce the fruit ourselves. He places the seed and cultivates it within each one of us. The fruit of spiritual transformation does not ripen overnight. It's a long and often difficult process. Some days I take one step forward only to take two steps backward the next day. Thankfully, the Holy Spirit is patient, very patient, with us.

Let's look at each fruit the Holy Spirit cultivates in us.

- Love: The love the Spirit produces isn't the feeling or emotional type of love. It's agape love. It's the respect and love for others—a sacrificial love—where we put others first, as Christ did when He died on the cross for our sins. "For God so loved the world, that he gave his only Son, that whoever believes in him should not perish but have eternal life" (John 3:16).

- Joy: Spirit-inspired joy is based on our inner contentment and peace, regardless of our physical circumstances. For example, we find joy in the Lord because He gives us the strength to get through any trial we face in life. In contrast, we may also find joy or happiness in eating our favorite snack, which is temporary and external. "Then he said to them, 'Go your way. Eat the fat and drink the sweet wine and send portions to anyone who has nothing ready, for this day is holy to our Lord. And do not be grieved, for the joy of the LORD is your strength' (Nehemiah 8:10).

- Peace: Peace tends to allude us when we live in world full of chaos. By seeking and finding the peace of Christ within us, we can reject that chaos and choose to live in harmony with others, as God intends for us to do. "Peace I leave with you; my peace I give to you. Not as the world gives do I give to you. Let not your hearts be troubled, neither let them be afraid" (John 14:27).

- Patience: Patience is not one of my strengths. Of all the fruit of the Spirit, this is the one that gives me the most trouble. We live in a fast-paced, want-it-right-now culture severely lacking in patience. However, through the Spirit, we can learn to be patient with others, as the Lord is patient with us. And boy, is He ever patient! "Be patient, therefore, brothers, until the coming of the Lord. See how the farmer waits for the precious fruit of the earth, being patient about it, until it receives the early and the late rains" (James 5:7).

- Kindness: Show kindness to others as God shows kindness to us through our salvation. Kindness is helping a person out by doing thoughtful deeds for them and not expecting something in return. It doesn't have to be a physical gift. It can be something as simple as smiling at someone who's had a rough day. That simple gesture could make another's day. "Put on then, as God's chosen ones, holy and beloved, compassionate hearts, kindness, humility, meekness, and patience (Colossians 3:12).

- Goodness: Goodness is showing generosity to others. Kindness and goodness go hand in hand. People can see the light of Christ shine through as the Spirit continues to grow and nourish his fruit in you. "Surely goodness and mercy shall follow me all the days of my life, and I shall dwell in the house of the LORD forever (Psalm 23:6).

- Faithfulness: Faithfulness is what Christ is to us. He is reliable and trustworthy, and we, in turn, can be so for Him. As our commitment toward our faith continues to cultivate and grow, we may find ourselves on the end of persecution—whether through actions or words on social media, we need to defend our faith and remain faithful to Christ. "For the LORD is good; his steadfast love endures forever, and his faithfulness to all generations" (Psalm 100:5).

- Gentleness: Gentleness is the opposite of selfishness. Finding strength in Christ will result in gentleness pouring out from us onto others. In a culture where it's all about me, gentleness demonstrates humility and meekness. As Christ offers His calming, reassuring gentleness to us, let us show that same gentleness to those around us. "Brothers, if anyone is caught in any transgression, you who are spiritual should restore him in a spirit of gentleness. Keep watch on yourself, lest you too be tempted (Galatians 6:1).

- Self-control: Self-control is the last of the fruit listed. Paul rounds out the fruit of the Spirit by circling back to "the works of the flesh" in Galatians 5:19–21. By practicing self-control, we are holding ourselves back from evil desires. Through the

Holy Spirit, we have the power and the ability to overcome the selfish desires we face daily. Praise the Lord for giving us this fruit! "A man without self-control is like a city broken into and left without walls (Proverbs 25:28).

While you and I face the daily pressures of the social media "perfect life" and our battle against the enemy of who we are in Christ, let's remember the Lord has provided the Holy Spirit to assist us in those daily battles.

As the Spirit cultivates our fruit, we continue to grow in Christ and cling tightly to who we are in Christ. Then the spiritual transformation we long for will begin to take place. We are a work in progress and one that the Lord will continue to love and tenderly care for. He will not leave or forsake us.

# CHAPTER 9

## BIBLICAL REFLECTION— MARY, THE MOTHER OF JESUS

*And when his parents saw him, they were astonished.*
*And his mother said to him,*
*"Son, why have you treated us so?*
*Behold, your father and I have been searching*
*for you in great distress."*
*And he said to them, "Why were you looking for me?*
*Did you not know that I must be in my Father's house?"*
Luke 2:48–49

She stood there in disbelief, tears streaming down her face, her body numb, and her heart crushed beyond repair. How was she ever going to get over this pain? How was she going to go on with her life? In a moment of human frailty, she may have even questioned God, "Why are you letting this happen, Lord?" As quickly as she may have thought that, she knew this was the Lord's plan all along. She understood and believed the Scriptures, and she knew that her son, nailed on that cross, was not just her son but *the Son,* the Son of the Father, the Savior, and the One who would pay the price for our sins.

She was the only person to witness both His birth *and* His death.

She's Mary, the Mother of Jesus.

## Indwelt with the Holy Spirit, Finding Favor in the Lord

Mary's story began when the angel Gabriel appeared to her and announced that she was the one the Lord had chosen to give birth to our Savior. Mary was the one who "had found favor in the Lord." Young and frightened, her only question was, "How will this be, since I am a virgin?" (Luke 1:34).

After an explanation from the angel, Mary accepted the gift the Lord chose her for. The next task was telling her fiancé, Joseph. In shock to find out that his beloved Mary was pregnant with a child from the Holy Spirit, Joseph reacted differently the way most men would. He sought a peaceful resolution.

Can you imagine that conversation between Mary and Joseph? In an era when stoning a woman for getting pregnant out of wedlock was acceptable, Joseph had compassion for Mary and was unwilling to put her to shame. He planned to divorce her quietly.

But God had other plans.

Enter Gabriel, the archangel, as he once again delivers a message from the Lord. This time it's to Joseph in a dream. Telling Joseph not to be afraid to take Mary as his wife, Gabriel emphasized that what Mary conceived was from the Holy Spirit and that she would bear a son. His name was to be Jesus. This child would save people from their sins, and this all would take place to fulfill the prophecies told by those who were entrusted by God to carry His message. Joseph awoke and immediately did what the angel told him to do. He married Mary and would raise the child as his own.

After giving birth to her son in her husband's hometown, Mary became a devoted mom. Following the customs of the day, she and Joseph took Jesus to the temple to present Him to the Lord (Luke 2:22–38). When the wise men came bearing gifts, she watched the visitors from the East worship her toddler son (Matthew 2:10–11), and she had a moment of panic when she couldn't find Jesus after attending the

Feast of the Passover (Luke 2:41–52). She was there at the beginning of her son's ministry, asking Him to turn water into wine at a wedding (John 2:1–11). If social media was available back then, she might have announced to the world how special her son was when He performed that miracle!

Mary was aware of all the teaching, miracles, and healing that Jesus was doing throughout the country. She had to have a sense of pride and jubilation as she watched her son, the Son of God, carry out the Father's plans.

The mother of Jesus also looked heartbreak straight in its face. She stood on the sidelines as she watched her oldest son ridiculed, persecuted, spat on, beat beyond recognition, mocked, and killed in one of the most humiliating, painful ways imaginable.

Nailed to the cross, Jesus looked down upon Mary with compassion. One of His final actions was to make sure His mother would be taken care of. He instructed John to care for her (John 19:26–27). Jesus then spoke His final words, "It is finished."

Mary was present when her son took His first breath and when He breathed His last.

And while the Bible doesn't explicitly state that Mary saw Jesus after His resurrection and ascension, she was with the other disciples and her sons as they waited for the Holy Spirit to come (Acts 1:14). She would have had to know that her son, our Savior, was resurrected from the dead.

## What We Can Learn from Mary

Mary was a sinner just like us, but she found favor with the Lord. And we do too. We have been given identities in Christ and the fruit of the Holy Spirit. The Lord is with us. While an angel may not appear to let us know exactly what to do (although that would be nice!), we have our Bibles to guide and direct us. We have the spirit of conviction that can turn us from our fleshly desires back toward Christ.

## Reflection and Journal Questions

1. What identities have you allowed to define you? What can you do to remind yourself of who you are in Christ?

2. If you are tired and burned out, prayerfully reflect on some of the reasons as to why you are. What steps can you take today to restart your walk with Jesus and get to know Him better?

3. Look at the list of the identity in Christ on page 51. Which of those do you believe about yourself? Which do you struggle to identify with?

4. Which fruit of the Spirit do you struggle with the most? How might you begin cultivating that fruit in your life?

# PART 3

## WHAT ARE THE SPIRITUAL HABITS?

*For the wages of sin is death,
but the free gift of God is eternal life
in Christ Jesus our Lord.*
Romans 6:23

# CHAPTER 10

## MY EXPERIENCE ENGAGING
## IN THE SPIRITUAL HABITS

*Therefore Eli said to Samuel, "Go, lie down,*
*and if he calls you, you shall say,*
*'Speak, LORD, for your servant hears.'"*
*So Samuel went and lay down in his place.*
*And the LORD came and stood,*
*calling as at other times, "Samuel! Samuel!"*
*And Samuel said, "Speak, for your servant hears."*
1 Samuel 3:9–10

The long, winding road took me back beyond what I'd imagined. There was no internet or cell phone coverage. I was indeed out in the boonies.

*Are you sure this is where I am supposed to be, Lord?* I questioned Him once again.

As I rounded the curve, a row of cabins, a swimming pool void of water, and the most beautiful reds, oranges, and yellows greeted me. The autumn silence filled this Christian summer camp. What a fitting response to my purpose in being there.

I'd received upsetting news a few days before I was set to arrive. This retreat was what I needed to drown my sorrows and have some quiet time. After years of being a stay-at-home mom, I stepped out in faith and applied for a writing position at a nationally known organization that served mothers of all ages. The position was located in a neighboring town—an easy drive from home—and the hours worked with my schedule. If I got the job, I could get paid to do what I loved: write. After two successful interviews, I felt confident I would be hired. Until one morning when I had a feeling in the pit of my stomach. You know the one that you get when something would not be turning out the way you had hoped. I heard the Holy Spirit whisper, "You didn't get the job." Sure enough, a few hours later I received a call with a friendly voice on the other end. "We've decided to go with someone else, but thank you for your interest."

The fear of failure and rejection swelled up in me, and I questioned if I even heard the Lord correctly. If I *did* hear Him correctly, then *why* didn't I get the job? Was it because my writing wasn't up to par? Was it my personality? Many questions entered my mind, and I didn't have the answers.

One of few benefits of Facebook is learning about events near me. In one post, the words *silence* and *solitude* retreat caught my eye. Ironically, it was posted by the president of the organization that didn't hire me. One of her friends was hosting a retreat, and she was spreading the word.

Silence and solitude were precisely what I needed after a rejection. Isn't that what most of us crave after a hard day or season? Time to process and think through things? I didn't even need to pray or think it over. Yes, this was the retreat for me, and maybe I could talk a friend into going. However, everyone was busy on the designated weekend. I would need to go alone.

## Alone but Not for Long

I will share a fun fact about myself. When I see an event that I am interested in attending and can't find a friend to go with me, I'll sign up and go by myself. I've gone to women and parent conferences, a photography conference, and a writer's conference without knowing a soul. Don't get me wrong, I love getting away for the weekend with a group of girlfriends, but there are times when I feel called to go somewhere and will go with or without a friend. The best part of going by myself is meeting other women who become lifelong friends.

This weekend was no exception. I went alone, and truthfully, a weekend of silence and solitude isn't meant for hanging out with friends. It's a time to sit and listen to the Lord and grow your faith.

Because the weekend was designed for participants to spend one-on-one time with the Lord, attendance was limited. Just as well, for if there were more attendees my focus may have been getting to know them better instead of growing closer to the Lord.

However, my nerves over not knowing anyone kicked in as I drove into the camp. I also began to question my hasty decision to attend this retreat. Perhaps I should have prayed more before signing up. What if the speaker said something that contradicted my Christian beliefs? Did the organizers promote the "faith and prosperity" gospel that is making such inroads in the church? The enemy used my fears against me, and I almost backed out.

Thank goodness I didn't.

I parked my total mom minivan and walked slowly to the retreat center. Grasping the doorknob, I opened the door only to be greeted by some of the friendliest women I have ever met. With opened arms and huge smiles, they put me at ease. I knew immediately that I was right where I needed to be after learning that I didn't get the job.

My original intent on participating in a silence and solitude retreat was because I needed to get away and recharge. As usual, though, the Lord had other plans for me. I sensed that the energy surrounding us in that cabin had been orchestrated by God, Himself.

The name of the retreat was exactly what it entailed. Friday evening through Sunday morning was silence and solitude. Following a schedule, we had times to visit with one another and times of quiet. And by quiet, I mean no talking at all. I'm an introvert by nature, and I enjoy the silence, but even I have my limits.

Based on Ruth Haley Barton's study, *Sacred Rhythms: Arranging Our Lives for Spiritual Transformation*, some of the spiritual habits were explained in greater detail. At this retreat the Lord took everything I thought I knew about spiritual transformation and spiritual habits, shook it up in a bottle, spilled it out in front of me, and said, "It's time to surrender completely to me!" It was at this time, I realized that spiritual transformation is more than accepting Christ as your Savior. It's a continual work in progress. We need to actively pursue a life like Christ daily. It was time for me to get serious.

How serious? For me, it was time to take the flame that was burning from the fire lit in the middle school parking lot and stoke it into a consuming fire. It was time to stop doing the minimal things and dig deeper into my relationship with Christ. In her book, Barton writes, "The stirring of spiritual desire indicates that God's spirit is already at work within us, drawing us to himself."[2]

If you are sensing the need for transformation, know that God is the one stirring that thirst for more. The seed is planted. It's time to water it so that it takes root in your soul.

# CHAPTER 11

## PUT THE PHONE DOWN

*And you shall love the Lord your God*
*with all your heart and with all your soul*
*and with all your mind and with all your strength.*
Mark 12:30

My retreat weekend revealed something I hadn't realized before.
My phone was an idol to me.

Thanks to no Wi-Fi or low cell signal, I couldn't check Facebook
or email. I could still send texts, so I made it a point to check in daily
with my family. I remember texting Craig that first night and telling
him how excited I was to be at the retreat, but I was also apprehen-
sive. Would I be able to focus solely on the Lord? Would I feel the
Holy Spirit as I walked through the trails throughout the campground?
More importantly, how would I ever get by without the full use of my
phone? At that moment I knew I needed to let go of the idols that filled
my silence and replace them with the whispers of the Holy Spirit.

Looking over my notes from that weekend, now over six years ago,
the first words I wrote were, "My heart and mind are open to you,
Jesus!" At the time, I knew that what I wanted most in this world
was a stronger relationship with Christ. I longed for more than what

I had. I wasn't talking about physical and material things but about a relationship with Christ so deep that when someone asked who my best friend was, I would say Jesus and my husband, Craig.

That weekend I soaked up everything I could and let the Lord do His work. And boy, did He ever! The weather was perfect, and the smell of autumn filled the air. God was at work because I finally tuned out the noise of the world and in my head. My focus was on the Word and Christ.

That's what we lack today, friends—silence.

We are bombarded with noise from the minute our feet hit the ground in the morning until we are tucked in at night. Raise your hand if you check Facebook before leaving your bed in the morning and before closing your eyes at night. I am raising both hands here because I've done it. Please know that I am not shaming you because I am guilty and continue to do so now and then. In fact, I did it this morning! It's a hard habit to break, but it can be broken. That retreat weekend reminded me of just how much I relied on my phone.

I reflected on the times I've waited in line at the grocery store or sat in the bleachers at a basketball game. My first impulse in such moments was to grab my phone and check my messages or social media. The phone had become an idol for me—one that isolated me from others. Look around the next time you are in public. How many people have their phones out? How many people are in their own little world and not noticing those around them?

We are much like the Israelites; our phones are the golden calves of today. The latest Android and iPhones aren't giant like a golden calf, but their allure is just as powerful.

After reading Exodus 32 numerous times over the years, I was struck by this revelation for the first time. Israel's episode with the golden calf was the result of their impatience. In the same way, we often experience impatience in our daily lives. We don't like to wait, and when we must, we don't know what to do with ourselves, so we grab our phones and mindlessly scroll through them without noticing what is going on around us.

The people of Israel grew weary of waiting for Moses to come down from the mountain where he was meeting with the Lord. On Mount Sinai, God communicated directly through Moses to the Israelites. The Ten Commandments—God's design for how his people should live together—were "written with the finger of God" (Exodus 31:18).

For whatever reason, the Israelites thought Moses was on the mountain too long and they became impatient. They needed to fill their time with something, anything, because they didn't like the silence. They wanted a god, any god who would go before them. Enter Aaron, the brother of Moses and the spokesperson for the Israelites. It was Aaron who delivered the Lord's messages to the Pharaoh. It was Aaron who held the staff that brought the plagues on the Egyptians; and it was Aaron who created the golden calf.

Yes, Moses's right-hand man caved to the people's pressure and shaped a cow out of gold that became Israel's idol.

I am a Christian, a child of God, and dedicated to furthering His kingdom, but a tablet the size of a 3x5 notecard turned into my idol.

If you cling to your phone a little too tightly, you are not alone. We all do it. From the two-year-old who is watching YouTube to keep quiet so mom can have a little peace to the 94-year-old man (my father-in-law!) who scours the local newspaper app, we all have an idol in our hands. If Aaron, a Levite priest, can cave to the Israelite's pressure and manufacture a fake cow with materials they gave him, a Christian woman can succumb to the latest social media craze.

So, what do we do? We put the device down and listen for the Lord to speak.

## In the Quiet, the Lord Speaks

After breakfast on our last day, I walked around the campground pond and found myself at the foot of a cross. It was a beautiful fall morning and the birds chirping and squirrels running through the woods comforted me. Sitting in silence, I heard the Holy Spirit whisper, "Your job right now is to be a stay-at-home mom; a time will come when a position will open that will fit your schedule better. Be patient."

75

Cue the tears.

A peace came over me. Without a doubt, I knew I was going to be okay.

One of the fears I faced that weekend was that as my children grew older, my role as a mom was diminishing. What would my future hold as I transitioned from the position of training to one of support and suggestions. It's a fear I am still working through, but I've been in tune with the Lord on what my calling is now.

My answer to what the Holy Spirit whispered came nine months later. I was offered a part-time job at the school my boys attended, and a few weeks after accepting that position, the organization that didn't hire me closed unexpectedly. Had I not been at the retreat and in tune with the Lord, I wouldn't have heard that sweet whisper of God's plans for me.

# CHAPTER 12

## PRACTICING SPIRITUAL HABITS LEADS TO SPIRITUAL TRANSFORMATION

*And we all, with unveiled face,*
*beholding the glory of the Lord,*
*are being transformed into the same image*
*from one degree of glory to another.*
*For this comes from the Lord who is the Spirit.*
2 Corinthians 3:18

*D*uring that first retreat, I learned how to start implementing different spiritual habits in my life. The spark of spiritual transformation began, but I needed to fuel it more. Spiritual transformation happens gradually. It doesn't happen overnight or even over a weekend. By practicing spiritual habits, transformation begins, and as Paul states in Romans 12:2, transformation takes place by the renewal of our minds. "Do not be conformed to this world, but be transformed by the renewal of your mind, that by testing you may discern what is the will of God, what is good and acceptable and perfect."

We need to focus and place in our minds the will to be transformed. We need to actively seek to be more like Christ. Transformation is hard and we cannot do it on our own. Barton writes, "I cannot transform myself, or anyone else for that matter. What I can do is create the conditions in which spiritual transformation can take place, by developing and maintaining a rhythm of spiritual practices that keep me open and available to God."[3]

Our first step is being open and available to God.

Since my first retreat, I make a point to attend some form of silence and solitude activity at least twice a year. Do I always hear from the Lord during these times? No, I don't. But it's not a total loss. Through Scripture the Lord reveals new insights to passages that I thought I knew, or a worship song becomes more meaningful because I slow down to listen to the words.

I still have my tear-stained journal from that weekend, and I read it regularly. It was a pivotal point in my spiritual transformation. We need times like this to recharge and refocus. We need to set our phones aside and pick up our Bibles. We need to listen for the Lord's whispers and act on them. Have you had the chance to just get away by yourself? I know that it's impossible at times even to have five minutes to yourself, but I highly encourage you to seek to do so. Regardless of what season of life we are in, if we spend time focusing on the things that draw us away from God, can we not also find a way to spend intentional time with God?

As I stated before, just because we participate in spiritual habits doesn't mean our lives will be perfect because all too often, just when I think that I am on the right path, my flesh overtakes me, and I take a step or two back. Just because I practice spiritual habits does not mean I am godly. They are a way to godliness, which has always been God's desire for us. We are made in God's image, but we are not God.

Since I began practicing spiritual habits, I have found myself in a pit of darkness many times. The heaviness of sin held me down, and the enemy enjoyed every minute of it. Even though I knew I needed to get out of the pit, at times I felt safer in that pit than I did out of it. The enemy was playing with me. "You enjoy what you are doing, even though you know that it is wrong! And besides, no one knows what you are doing, so just stay where you are!" And so, I did. Until one day, the Holy Spirit grabbed me by the shirt collar and lifted me out of the pit. The Lord fought for me, and He will fight for you (Exodus 14:14).

Once out of the pit, I returned to the spiritual habits. I steered clear of the triggers that got me in the pit in the first place. If you are struggling with an issue of deep sin, I am here to tell you that you will get out. It takes work, but you will feel the Holy Spirit grab you by the collar and hoist you out of the pit.

Looking back on your life and your past regrets or mistakes, you may be led to believe that you cannot be spiritually transformed. That is the enemy feeding you lies. As the old saying goes, "When the enemy reminds you of your past, remind him of his future."

# CHAPTER 13

## BIBLICAL REFLECTION— THE APOSTLE PAUL

*But Saul increased all the more in strength,*
*and confounded the Jews who lived in Damascus*
*by proving that Jesus was the Christ.*
Acts 9:22

Wen it comes to a radical spiritual transformation, one name comes to mind.

Saul, sweet Saul. Or should I say, Paul, sweet Paul? Many of us are familiar the story of Paul and his conversion, but after more study, I've discovered some things that I had overlooked.

I use Saul and Paul interchangeably throughout this section. Here is a bit of trivia to use at your next Starbucks meetup with your friends. Contrary to what we may think, God did not change Saul's name to Paul after that life-changing day on the road to Damascus. Saul was Paul's Jewish name, and Paul was Saul's Greek name. No verse in the New Testament says, "And God changed Saul's name to Paul after his life-altering events on the road to Damascus."

Mind blown.

Born in Tarsus to Jewish parents, he was a Roman citizen—a fact he capitalized on during his ministry, especially when persecuted. His father was a Pharisee. Following in his father's footsteps, Paul studied under the great Gamaliel. He knew the law and the Torah exceptionally well. He paid close attention to those around him, making sure the people adhered to those laws.

Imagine Saul's emotions when he saw the "radical" Christians challenging the old way of things. The extreme hatred he must have felt to see baptisms in the name of Christ. And he was seeing these Christ-followers healing and preaching. How absurd!

Saul did what every hotheaded, by-the-book person did. He took matters into his own hands. Paul did what a lot of us do when we feel our lives are out of control; he tried to regain control with his own power. He authorized the execution of Christians. Saul saw to it that these new, transformed Christians paid for their words and actions.

Stephen, the first martyred believer, cried out to God as he was being stoned. Paul's companion Luke pens these verses:

> But he, full of the Holy Spirit, gazed into heaven and saw the glory of God, and Jesus standing at the right hand of God. And he said, "Behold, I see the heavens opened, and the Son of Man standing at the right hand of God." But they cried out with a loud voice and stopped their ears and rushed together at him. Then they cast him out of the city and stoned him. And the witnesses laid down their garments at the feet of a young man named Saul. And as they were stoning Stephen, he called out, "Lord Jesus, receive my spirit." And falling to his knees, he cried out with a loud voice, "Lord, do not hold this sin against them." And when he had said this, he fell asleep (Acts 7:55–60).

As often as I read these verses, the same thought occurs to me. Why didn't someone step in and help Stephen? Surely, someone in the crowd knew this was wrong. Perhaps they felt if they spoke up, they would be placing themselves in the same situation that Stephen found himself in.

Saul, being a Pharisee, could have also stopped this atrocity. He knew the Lord forbade murder. And yet, he decided to go with the mob mentality and allow the senseless death to happen.

One would think the following verse would say, "And Saul, realized his mistake and asked God for forgiveness." Nope. He doesn't even flinch or show remorse. Saul shed no tears. Rather, he continued "ravaging the church, and entering house after house, he dragged off men and women and committed them to prison" (Acts 8:3).

Unfortunately, this attack on the church is still occurring today. We still see news stories about people getting attacked and dragged from their homes. While it's not prevalent here in the United States, in countries such as China, Iran, and Iraq, persecution of Christians is a common occurrence.

And it all started with Saul.

Saul's rampage did not go unnoticed. Enter the road to Damascus. If we were watching this unfold on the big screen, there would be suspenseful music as a big, bright light and the booming voice of our Savior met Saul on that road.

Saul's instant reaction was to fall as he heard the voice of our Savior, "Saul, Saul, why are you persecuting me?" I love how often the Lord Jesus calls out names twice. Something important is coming up, so you'd better listen. It's like your mom calling you by your first and middle name. We are at full attention when we hear those words.

"Who are you, Lord?" Saul quickly replied.

"I am Jesus, whom you are persecuting. But rise and enter the city, and you will be told what you are to do." (Scene taken from Acts 9:4-6, author's paraphrase.)

Notice Jesus didn't say, "I am Jesus, and you are persecuting my followers." He said that Saul was actually persecuting Jesus.

Saul's traveling companions stood there speechless—stunned by this supernatural event. I can't help but wonder why Saul questioned who he was speaking to. He knew the Torah, so he would have known that the Lord uses light to get His message across. Although Jesus doesn't communicate today with lights and a booming voice, He does use the Holy Spirit to prompt and nudge us.

Saul's companions brought him to the city of Damascus as Jesus commanded. For three days, Saul didn't eat or drink. I often wonder what was going through Saul's mind at this point. One could say he was practicing the spiritual habit of fasting.

We meet Ananias, a disciple whom the Lord uses as part of Saul's transformation. In a vision, the Lord instructs him to go and help Saul. "Rise and go to the street called Straight, and at the house of Judas look for a man of Tarsus named Saul for behold, he is praying, and he has seen in a vision a man named Ananias come in and lay his hands on him so that he might regain his sight" (Acts 9:11–12).

Ananias says, "Hold up! Hang on! Something's not right here!" (my paraphrase). He's heard of Saul's rampage and is aware of the extreme hatred that Saul had toward Christians. He knew the evil that Saul had done and how the chief priests gave him the authority to bind all new believers who call on the name of the Lord. At this point, I can't help but wonder if Ananias thought he heard the Lord correctly.

How many times do we question the Holy Spirit? When we feel the prompting to take a step of faith, try something new, or even help a stranger out, how often do we question if that is really what God wants us to do? I often question before I listen. I'm a work in progress, and I hope and pray that I will automatically do what the Lord is prompting me to do without question one day.

Reassuring our new friend, the Lord spoke these words, "Go, for he is a chosen instrument of mine to carry my name before the Gentiles and kings and the children of Israel. For I will show him how much he must suffer for the sake of my name" (Acts 9:15–16).

That's all the convincing that Ananias needed. He went to Saul, laid his hands on him, and said, "Brother Saul, the Lord Jesus who appeared to you on the road by which you came has sent me so that you may regain your sight and be filled with the Holy Spirit" (Acts 9:17, author's paraphrase). Immediately the scales fell from Saul's eyes, and he regained his sight.

The following simple but powerful sentence brings tears to my eyes, "He rose and was baptized; and taking food, he was strengthened" (Acts 9:18b–19).

The first thing Paul did when he regained sight wasn't to seek out food. It was to declare publicly that he was a follower of Christ. Talk about a complete turnabout! The man who once persecuted Christians was now a Christian himself. A spiritual transformation took place that rocked his world.

We know that he didn't have an easy life after his conversion based on his own writings. Beaten, stoned, tortured, imprisoned, and chained to a Roman soldier are some of the things he endured. Just as the Lord told Ananias, "For I will show him how much he must suffer for the sake of my name" (Acts 9:16).

This applies to us also, friends.

We all, in various degrees, must be prepared to suffer for the sake of Jesus's name.

We know that Paul suffered throughout his lifetime. He penned many letters to the churches while chained to a Roman soldier in a dark, damp cell. The letters to Timothy are believed to be written shortly before his death. While we may not be executed for our beliefs, we may be judged, censored, and cursed for being followers of Christ, especially on social media.

Do not let that stop you from living a full life in Christ. You are reading this book because you are yearning for a change. You love Jesus, but sometimes the world gets the best of you. It also gets the best of me. Thankfully, we have a loving Savior who knows what it's like to live in this world. We are not alone.

# Reflection and Journal Questions

1. When you hear the words *spiritual disciplines*, what is the first thought that comes to your mind and why?

2. Do you struggle with silence? If you do, you are not alone. What are some steps you can take today to begin practicing silence and solitude?

3. Look at your phone. Is it something you cling to? When you have downtime, do you scroll mindlessly through the apps? Carefully pray about why you do this and how you can spend less time on your phone. Write your ideas on a post-it note to remind yourself to put your phone down and enjoy the life the Lord intends for you to live.

4. What part of Paul's story resonates the most with you? Reflecting on your life, write a note thanking Jesus for all that He has done for you. Whatever happened in the past is in the past, and your sins are forgiven. You are made new again! Praise Jesus for His everlasting love for you!

# PART 4

# THE
# SPIRITUAL
# HABITS

*Now Jesus was praying in a certain place,*
*and when he finished, one of his disciples said to him,*
*"Lord, teach us to pray, as John taught his disciples."*
*And he said to them, "When you pray, say:*
*"Father, hallowed be your name. Your kingdom come.*
*Give us each day our daily bread, and forgive us our sins,*
*for we ourselves forgive everyone who is indebted to us.*
*And lead us not into temptation."*
Luke 11:1–4

# CHAPTER 14

## THE SPIRITUAL HABIT OF PRAYER

*Rejoice always, pray without ceasing,*
*give thanks in all circumstances;*
*for this is the will of God*
*in Christ Jesus for you.*
1 Thessalonians 5:16–18

How is your prayer life? Please put some serious thought into that question. I'm asking this not to make anyone feel any guilt or shame, because I, too, have struggled with finding some one-on-one time with Jesus. Despite my attempts to rein in my activities, many days I still feel like I'm being pulled in twenty different directions—at the same time. Maybe you can relate? Our days are filled with getting our children fed and clothed and driving them around to different sports and activities. Our jobs require our undivided attention, but it's hard when we are exhausted. Regardless of the pace of our lives, an established prayer time is an essential practice in spiritual transformation.

Not only will regular prayer time bring you closer to Jesus, but those around you will also benefit from the time you spend in prayer.

So, to repeat the question, how is your prayer life?

Is it nonexistent? Are you waiting to find the perfect pen and journal in which to jot your prayers? Or are you too tired, too busy, or too whatever? Maybe you feel as if your words are not eloquent enough to pray to God.

You hear other women pray with such confidence and boldness. Knowing you can't do the same, you keep quiet. Afraid of hemming and hawing or stammering, you pray silently. Perhaps you don't have any Bible verses memorized to throw in the middle of your prayer like your friends do. Instead of embarrassing yourself, you stay quiet and mutter an amen at an appropriate time.

Perhaps, you struggle with prayer because you have no idea where to even begin.

In the past, I've used each of these excuses for not setting aside time to pray. However, my main excuse was, "Why bother if the Lord doesn't answer my prayers?"

I am so thankful that God is a patient, loving God, because many times I envisioned God sighing and shaking His head in disgust, saying, "Seriously, Missy? You've seen what I've done in your life thus far, and you still don't believe that I answer your prayers? Come on!"

God isn't sitting on His throne looking down on us with judgment. He yearns for communication from His children, and that's exactly what prayer is—children talking to their Father. Foster writes, "Prayer is the central avenue God uses to transform. . . . The closer we come to the heartbeat of God, the more we see our need and the more we desire to be conformed to Christ."[4]

Prayer transforms us.

## Our Savior Prayed

Jesus is an excellent example of living the life of prayer. Prayer was an essential part of His ministry. If Jesus, the Son of God, made prayer a priority in His life, we can also make it a priority.

After His baptism, Jesus prayed, and the heavens were opened (Luke 3:21). After a busy day of healing and teaching, Jesus got up early and prayed (Mark 1:35). The night before He chose the twelve apostles, He went out to the mountain and prayed all night (Luke 6:12–13). Before walking on water, He was alone in prayer (Matthew 14:23–25). Jesus was in prayer before the apostle Peter confessed that Jesus was "the Christ of God" (Luke 9:18–20). Jesus took Peter, James, and John on the mountain to pray, and the transfiguration occurred (Luke 9:28–31). Lazarus was buried for three days before Jesus arrived at his tomb, and standing before it, the Messiah prayed before the dead man walked out of His tomb (John 11:41–42). Parents brought their children to Him, so He might lay His hands on them and pray over them (Matthew 19:13–15).

During Holy Week, Scripture records Jesus prayed at critical points. These occasions were essential in preparing Him for what lay ahead. He prayed a blessing over the bread at the Last Supper (Matthew 26:26). Jesus told him that He prayed specifically that Peter's faith not fail after Satan demanded to have Peter so that he might sift him like wheat (Luke 22:31–32). Before going to the garden of Gethsemane, He prayed for Himself, His apostles, and for all believers (John 17:1–26). In Gethsemane, Jesus prayed three specific prayers before being betrayed by Judas and handed over to the Jews (Matthew 26:36–46). After He was nailed to the cross, He prayed for the people who were crucifying Him (Luke 23:34). While dying, He prayed to the Father, "My God, My God, why have you forsaken me?" (Matthew 27:46). And in His dying breath, our Savior prayed, "Father, into your hands I commit my spirit!" (Luke 23:46).

This is not, however, the end of the story, and it's not the end of Jesus's praying to God and over His disciples. On that glorious third day, Jesus Christ rose from the grave, establishing that not even death can keep Him down.

After the resurrection, Jesus prayed a blessing before breaking bread and eating with His disciples (Luke 24:30). And finally, He prayed one final prayer over His followers before ascending into heaven (Luke 24:50–51).

As Whitney wrote, "If Jesus needed to pray, how much more do we need to pray? Prayer is expected of us because we need it. We will not be like Jesus without it."[5]

## Be Careful What You Pray For!

"I cannot believe that You are making me do this! I'm not talking to her if she is with someone!" I muttered to God as I grasped the handle and swung open the door to the church lobby. The rattle from the metal doorjamb caused innocent bystanders to stop and stare.

I didn't care what they thought. I wanted to find this woman, do what I came to do, and go about my evening. Tears filled my eyes as I scanned the room. I hoped and prayed that I heard the Lord wrong, but I knew in my heart I'd heard Him correctly. The tightness in my chest confirmed this.

With no sign of her, I sighed with relief and turned around to head back to my car. That's when I spotted her, sitting by herself, just as the Lord had planned it all along.

With a deep breath and much apprehension, I tearfully walked up to this stranger and, with a trembling voice, said, "This is going to sound weird, but the Lord has prompted me to pray for you. Are you in need of prayer?"

She glanced at me and without hesitation, softly said, "Yes."

At that very moment, the tightness in my chest went away.

A few weeks before this encounter, I had felt a stirring in my heart to help a stranger. What would happen if I did what the Holy Spirit nudged me to do as soon as I felt prompted? No questions asked, no doubting my ability, just following directions from the Lord?

So, I prayed, "Lord, please lead me to a person who needs my help. Please give me the courage to step out of my comfort zone and be obedient to Your directions."

It was a prayer that I thought would be answered by a "pay it forward" in the drive-through line or by helping someone who had physical needs.

Never would I have thought it was to pray in public for a stranger. Praying in public is not one of my strengths, but that evening, the Lord not only provided the words for me to say but gave me the courage to do it.

## Prayer is a Never-Ending Journey

I've come a long way in my prayer journey. I've tried certain practices and techniques. I've read book after book on prayer. While there is nothing wrong with reading about the subject of prayer, the problem for me was taking time to implement the practices that I read about and apply them to my lackluster prayer life. Reading about prayer and participating in prayer are two different things. I finally decided to stop the research and just do it.

## There is No Wrong Way to Pray, Just Do It!

One of my struggles at the beginning of my journey in prayer was not knowing where to begin. Questions of doubt and my inability to pray fervently stood as a roadblock to my spiritual transformation. It finally dawned on me that God wants me to spend time with Him. He's not looking for some specific, "If you don't pray this way, I'm not listening to you" prayer. He wants an uninterrupted time with me. He wants me to focus solely on Him. He wants me to bring my worries and anxieties to Him. He wants me to talk to Him because He loves and cares for me.

If you are not engaging in an active prayer life because you don't know how to pray, you are giving the enemy a foothold in your life. Take a moment to think about this. The enemy is loving that you are not talking with God. He loves the fact that our lives are so busy that we put others in front of the Lord. We are in a spiritual battle. Paul writes in Ephesians 6:10–12, "Finally, be strong in the Lord and in the strength of his might. Put on the whole armor of God, that you may be able to stand against the schemes of the devil. For we do not wrestle against flesh and blood, but against the rulers, against the authorities, against the cosmic powers over this present darkness, against the spiritual forces of evil in the heavenly places."

The enemy wants nothing more than to distance us from our heavenly Father.

One approach to prayer is using the acronym ACTS: Adoration, Confession, Thanksgiving, Supplication and Silence. If, like me, you struggle with getting started, ACTS is the solution. I came across this way of praying when I attended my first Moms in Prayer (then called Moms in Touch). It is a unique and simple way of structuring your daily prayers.

## A Is for Adoration

Begin your prayer time by focusing on the attributes or characteristics of God. Worship the Lord by acknowledging his greatness: Almighty, Counselor, Deliverer, Faithful, Father, Holy, King, Lord Most High, Prince of Peace, Provider, Rock, and Shield are just a few words speaking to His greatness.

One of my favorite words to attribute to God is *Jehovah*. This is translated as the true, eternal God and the great I AM. The Christian recording artists Phillips, Craig, and Dean recorded a song entitled "Great I Am." If you are struggling to get in the right mindset for prayer, I encourage you to listen to this song. Meditate on the words, and in no time, you will be praising the Lord as the great I AM !

An example of a prayer of adoration is, "God and Father Almighty, I praise You because You are my comforter and protector . . ." or "Jehovah, You are the Light of the World and my strength . . ."

## C Is for Confession

After praising the Lord for who He is, it's time for a confession. Confessing our sins is personal, it is between you and the Lord. Our faithful Father has opened the lines of forgiveness through the death of His Son, our Savior, on the cross. In Old Testament times, burnt and blood sacrifices were offered as an act of confession for the sins of the people.

Jesus atoned for our sins through His death, burial, and resurrection. Confessing our sins may feel uncomfortable. Rehashing our not-so-good choices or actions might make us feel that we are unworthy of the love of God. However, remember the truth. We are not unworthy in His eyes. We are loved, and we are forgiven. Never forget that!

In confession, we are invited to be specific. We can bare it all to God—our judgmental attitudes, jealousy, anger, selfishness, and whatever else stands in the way of leading the life God wants us to have.

Once we confess our sins, we are forgiven. First John 1:9 says, "If we confess our sins, he is faithful and just to forgive us our sins and to cleanse us from all unrighteousness." The enemy tries his best to bring them to mind again and to shame us again for sins that have already been confessed. Do not listen to him! Our sins are at the feet of the Savior on the cross! Your future is eternal life with Christ. The enemy's fate is eternal damnation, and he knows it.

I love the New Living Translation of Psalm 103:12, "He has removed our sins as far from us as the east is from the west." Listen to the Casting Crowns song, "East to West," if you need more of a reminder that your sins are removed. This is the time to focus on the Word of God and nothing else.

## T Is for Thanksgiving

Thanksgiving follows confession. Now is the time to thank God for what He has done in your life.

Thank Him for answered prayers.

Thank Him for the people in your life.

You can thank God for just about everything in your life, from the answered prayer for healing of a loved one or friend to thanking God that you found your keys and weren't late getting your children to school on time.

The Bible contains verse after verse thanking the Lord for His love, protection, and guidance. One of my favorites is found in 1 Chronicles 16:34, "Oh give thanks to the Lord, for he is good; for his steadfast love endures forever!"

## S Is for Supplication and Silence

After thanksgiving, it's time for supplication—make your requests known to God by lifting up prayers for yourself and others. We've spoken words of adoration, confessed our sins, and thanked God for answered prayers and what He has done in our lives. Now it's time to make our requests.

Use this time not only to lift up your family and friends but also to pray for yourself. Let me repeat that: It's okay to pray for yourself, friends!

If you are a mom, you know that, we tend to put our children before ourselves and our needs. From birth to the time they launch out on their own, our children are our number one priority. We've lost sleep, shed tears, and even shared the last bite of our favorite ice cream with them—and wait until they are teenagers and you don't even have a chance to eat your favorite ice cream because they will eat it before we can! It's right and understandable to make your children a top priority. That is in our nature. However, we also need to take care of ourselves. So, it's okay to pray for yourself, even if it's just a simple prayer not to get upset when you help your child with their math homework!

I cannot stress enough how important it is to pray for your family. We live in a sinful world where our children and family members are bombarded daily with the pressures of the world. Do not believe that your prayers will not matter! The Lord will hear your prayers, so lift your family up to Him daily!

You can also use this time to petition for friends and family, church leaders, and the leaders in our government. If time is limited, choose a day of the week to pray for others specifically. For example, every Monday you might pray for your children's school administration and teachers. On Tuesdays you would specifically pray for your church pastor, elders, and leaders. Wednesday's prayer focus could be on your coworkers. Thursday's prayer focus would be on a ministry that you support, and Friday would be an "open forum" prayer day.

The important thing to remember is that there is no right or wrong way to pray. The Lord wants to hear from us! The lines of communication are always open, and nothing pleases the Lord more than His children coming to Him in prayer.

After supplication, it's time to sit in silence and listen to God.

Listen for anything the Lord wants you to hear. This will not be in the form of a big, booming voice that you see depicted in the movies.

Although, I have to admit that would be nice at times! It may be a whisper or a sense of peace and calmness. Often times, thoughts enter my mind that I know could have only been the Lord whispering to me. You may even feel the Spirit stirring inside you. Savor this quiet time with the Lord!

Don't be discouraged if you don't hear from the Lord. At times you may sit in silence and not hear or feel anything from the Lord. That's okay. Keep feeding your soul with prayer. I can go weeks at a time with silence, but I know that He hears my prayers, and He is with me—just as He is with you!

As you commit to spending daily time with the Lord, you will find your faith grow stronger by the day. Your soul will be refreshed, and you will be able to handle whatever the world hands you that day. We live in a fallen world, and our days will not be perfect. However, if I start my day with the Lord, I will feel more prepared for anything that comes at me during the day.

You may be thinking to yourself, *Well, that's just all fine and dandy for you to get up early in the morning, but I'm not a morning person. How can I apply this to my situation?*

The answer is simple. Find a time that fits your current stage of life. If you are a night person, your prayer time may be after the kids go to bed. If you work full-time, you may use your lunch hour as your prayer time. Morning, noon, or night—it doesn't matter! The Lord is waiting and willing to meet you, so please make it a priority to meet with Him.

It's important to make an active commitment to prayer time. Speaking from experience, prayer time is a sacrifice. There may be times when you just want to binge-watch Netflix, but you feel the Holy Spirit nudging you that it's time for some one-on-one time with God. Put the remote down, turn off the TV, and grab your Bible and notebook. Netflix—and anything else—will be waiting for you after your prayer time.

## Joining Others in Prayer

Once you establish a personal prayer time for yourself, you may feel inclined to join others in prayer. I encourage you to invite a few friends and create your own small group. With the assurance that prayer requests remain confidential, pray for each other's needs. If you can't meet in person, various apps and video technology enables us to meet remotely with a small group of believers.

Another option is joining a Moms in Prayer group. Moms worldwide meet weekly in private and public schools to pray over their children and school. Not only is this a great way to meet other moms in your children's classes, but you also have other moms to walk beside you in your journey of motherhood. As my children have grown older and are in their late teens, I am grateful that MIP also serves those of us with college age and early career children.

I will never forget the first time I attended a MIP meeting at my children's school. We had moved to the area only a few months earlier, and I didn't know a soul. I met moms that are still my friends today, friends that I can always text when I need prayers over my teenagers.

My friend, Nicole, leads my local group, and here is her perspective on how Moms in Prayer impacted her life. She writes:

> When my oldest was a first grader, I asked God to give me opportunities for deep conversations with other moms at school. I yearned for more than the superficial conversations that can happen in the student pickup line after school. God saw I needed more deep conversation and answered abundantly. He led me to Moms in Prayer. There is something very beautiful that God does when women pray together. The Holy Spirit does great work. He has knitted us in a way that friendships develop. These women have lifted me up and prayed when my heart felt helpless. They have lifted up my kids when I don't know what to pray anymore. They

have walked alongside me, prayed, and encouraged me in the difficult journey of mothering through these many years. Moms in Prayer has given me a tool to pray. While there is no one specific way to pray, I have learned that the four steps of prayer not only guide my mind but prepare my heart to pray to the Lord with others. Starting with praise takes my mind off of my worries and agenda. Praise reminds me of how big our great God is. Confession brings me even closer to Him and reminds me of my position and my daily need to remember the gospel. Thanksgiving reveals the bounty of blessings the Lord brings to me, my family, and all of us praying. Supplication then naturally follows those steps. Beyond our MIP group, I have grown closer to the Lord as a result of praying using the four steps of prayer. The Lord has brought me to be a co-leader of our school's MIP group. I have had opportunities to teach a five-day class about prayer to high school students. MIP has been a catalyst in learning more and more about how the Lord uses prayer to deepen my relationship with Him and to deepen my relationship with women. He is teaching me through His Word and through prayer time the great power of prayer. That our prayers unleash His power. Our time spent with Him in prayer changes me. It can turn worry into praise. It can take worry and turn it into a beautiful testimony of God's faithfulness. I asked the Lord to give me deeper friendships. He answered above and beyond my request.[6]

If your child's school doesn't have a Moms in Prayer group, talk with your school administration and start one. Get the word out that prayer is essential, and you all will be meeting to lift your children to the Lord. If the Spirit is stirring, moms will come.

One final word on prayer from one of my favorite authors, Timothy Keller. In his book, *Prayer: Experiencing Awe and Intimacy with God,* he writes, "Prayer is awe, intimacy, struggle—yet the way to reality. There is nothing more important, or harder, or richer, or more life-altering. There is absolutely nothing so great as prayer."[7]

# CHAPTER 15

# THE SPIRITUAL HABIT OF MEDITATION

*This Book of the Law*
*shall not depart from your mouth,*
*but you shall meditate on it day and night,*
*so that you may be careful to do*
*according to all that is written in it.*
Joshua 1:8

*W*hat is the first thing you think of when you hear the word *meditation?*

For me, an image of a person sitting on the floor, back straight, legs crossed, and hands either resting on the knees or together forming a prayer-like posture comes to mind.

This is Eastern meditation. Yoga and New Age practices use these forms of meditation. Eastern meditation requires a person to empty themselves of the daily drudge of life and clear the mind. Christian meditation fills the mind with God and His truths.

Eastern meditation's focus is to detach from the world and empty our minds.

Christian meditation's focus is to attach to God and fill our minds with God's Word and truth.

In *Spiritual Disciplines for the Christian Life*, Donald Whitney writes this: "Let's define meditation as deep thinking on truths and spiritual realities revealed in Scripture, or upon life from a spiritual perspective, for the purposes of understanding, application, and prayer."[8] Foster writes, "Christian meditation leads us to the inner wholeness necessary to give ourselves to God."[9]

Throughout the Bible, we see examples of God's children practicing meditation. The prophets Eli, Samuel, Elijah, Isaiah and Jeremiah, King David, and Jesus all practiced this spiritual habit.

Meditation and memorizing Scripture can go hand in hand. Meditating on Scripture lends itself to memorization. This comes in handy when you are in prayer or need a spiritual boost to get through the worst days.

Let's look at some of the ways to meditate on Scripture. These are only suggestions, and you can try as many as you like until you find the one that works best for you. The key is not to be overwhelmed. As we discuss the various meditation techniques, remember this is between you and the Lord. No one will be looking over your shoulder and telling you that you are not doing it right.

## Meditating through Scripture

This is my favorite form of meditation and the one I used to get through a challenging time for our family. The week before my son's surgery, I began meditating on Isaiah 41:10, "Fear not, for I am with you; be not dismayed, for I am your God; I will strengthen you, I will help you, I will uphold you with my righteous right hand."

I chose this verse because I knew that my son needed to be prayed over, and he needed the strength to get through this particular surgery. He was afraid, and as a mom, I did everything I could to alleviate that fear. I wrote the verse on notecards and placed them around the house in areas where I spend the most time. I taped it to my computer, placed one above the kitchen sink, stuck one to my car dashboard, and put one on my bathroom mirror. During my quiet time, I sat in silence, meditating on each word like the rabbit chewing methodically on the carrots in our garden. He was determined to eat them all, and I was determined to be armed with the Word, praying this verse over my son.

Connor was born with *pectus excavatum*, a genetic condition that creates a funnel in the chest cavity. My husband and oldest son have this also, but theirs are minor. Connor's condition was noticeable right after he was born. Our pediatrician informed us that the indent was profound, and surgery would be required when he was in his teens to correct the problem.

Connor lived a relatively normal life until seventh grade. Due to excessive adolescent growth, his chest's deformity had grown so deep that it was affecting his heart and lung function. It seemed as if this happened overnight. One night Connor was running up and down the basketball court like any normal player, and the next game he was so out of breath that he could only make it down the court for a few minutes at a time. Even the simple task of walking down the hall made him short of breath. Seeing my son like this brought me to tears. As much as I requested him to sit out the rest of the season, his mind was set on finishing it. Connor and his coaches developed a system: he would pull on his jersey when he was struggling to breathe, signaling to the coaches that he needed to sit down for a few minutes. He finished the season, and fear of the surgery loomed over him.

Although the surgery only takes about forty-five minutes, it is invasive. It requires a metal bar be inserted between the breastplate and vital organs and tightened to "pop" his chest up, thus relieving the pressure on those organs.

Armed with my Bible and journal, I sat in a corner of the waiting room and meditated on Isaiah 41:10 over and over. *Don't be afraid, Connor. God is with you. He will strengthen you. He will uphold you with His righteous hand.*

The surgery went as planned, and Connor's pain was manageable until the second night of our hospital stay.

If you have ever had a medical procedure, you know the day after surgery, the pain can be some of the worst. At this point in recovery, the anesthesia wears off, and regular doses of pain medicine are intended to relieve the discomfort. However, every breath, slight movement, cough, or sneeze can be agonizing until the body heals.

For Connor, this hit at 1:30 in the morning.

"Mom, I can't do this anymore!" He moaned in intense pain.

Standing by his hospital bed and tightly holding his hand, I did the only thing I knew to do—pray. "Please, Lord, let the pain medicine start working!" I cried out.

"God, please help me!" Connor whispered. Hearing my son crying out to the Great Physician brought me to tears.

"Yes, Connor, focus on God! He will get you through this!" I said.

Now all that meditating on Isaiah 41:10 before, during, and after the surgery became important. At this moment of sheer pain, Connor needed that verse more than ever.

A moment when the pain was unbearable.

A moment when a mother stood helpless.

A moment when a boy cried out to God.

A moment when a mother doubted if God heard that cry. That's right; I doubted God. If He did hear our prayers, why was my son still in pain?

I whispered the same meditation as I did in the waiting room. *Don't be afraid, Connor. God is with you. He will strengthen you. He will uphold you with His righteous hand.*

Immediately after that thought, Connor looked at me and said, "The pain is almost gone!" We both knew that while the medicine played a role, the Lord was the ultimate Pain Reducer.

Thirty minutes after speaking that verse, Connor was asleep, and I asked God for forgiveness. In a moment of panic and fear, I had chosen to rely on my strength and not on God alone. In times of distress, the Lord is there to uphold, help, and strengthen us.

By meditating on this verse before the surgery, I was able to use it to calm Connor down by praying it over him. Those words brought comfort to him when he needed it the most.

The surgery was the easy part. The eight weeks of recovery was one of the most challenging seasons for our family. We clung tightly to Isaiah 41:10, and together with the Lord's help, we were able to conquer the enemy's attacks and assist Connor on his path to healing. The day after the surgeon cleared Connor, he was back out on the soccer field, breathing freely and free of pain.

## Take a Walk

Another form of meditation is walking while focusing spiritually on God's creation. Locally, we have a nature center that I love to walk through, and I am in awe to see the Lord at work throughout this little piece of heaven in the midst of the city.

In Illinois, we get our fair share of cold and snow during the winter. As the winter drags on, I grow weary. However, after every significant winter event, the snow blankets the ground, creating a welcome silence.

It's breathtaking.

Under the cloud-covered skies and inches of snow, God is making things new again!

During the spring months, I focus on the new growth taking place as nature emerges from its winter hibernation. The trees begin to bud, bluebells start to bloom, the grass turns green again, and the songbirds return from their winter migration.

Summer brings out deer, squirrels, chipmunks, and occasional wild turkeys. More people are out and about on the trails, and the sun brings on a cheerful, happy attitude.

The autumn months bring the vibrant colors of yellow, red, and orange leaves. The Lord truly puts the most beautiful colors on display to remind us that beauty is in our lives, no matter what we are facing.

I encourage you to take time and focus on God's handiwork that surrounds your environment. Take a walk, give thanks for what He has given you, and meditate on the beauty that surrounds you.

## Focus on Each Word or Phase of the Verse Individually

Another great way to meditate on Scripture is to take a verse and focus on each individual word. For example, let's take Psalm 46:10 and focus on each phrase. "Be still, and know that I am God."

*Be still.* As you meditate on this, ask the Lord to help you be still and quiet your mind.

*Be still, and know.* As you continue, ask the Lord to reveal what He wants you to know about Him and His wonders.

*Be still, and know that I am God.* Wrap up your meditation time knowing that He is the Lord of Lord's and He is in control.

Prayerfully consider which verses to meditate on. You will be in awe as the Holy Spirit reveals the verse that you need at the exact moment you need it.

## Write the Bible Verse in Your Own Words or Paraphrase

Did you know that by writing out a Bible verse, you will remember it better? In a world where keyboards have replaced handwriting, handwriting is slowly becoming a lost art. Even in our schools, students as young as kindergarten use some form of electronic device to do their school and homework.

I am currently enrolled in graduate classes to obtain a Certificate in Spiritual Formation, and I'm one of the few who doesn't use a computer to take notes. Please know that I am not putting anyone down for using this method. For me, it's better to write out what I read and see in my own words and handwriting. This helps me retain information better.

Paraphrasing a verse or section of verses is an effective form of meditation as it focuses our thoughts on the verse and allows more time to ponder its meaning and consider how to apply it to our life. We must take care not to paraphrase the verse into our voice, or misconstrue or rewrite the verse in a way that gives it a completely different meaning than the Lord intends. We are learners of the Bible, not rewriters of the Bible.

Here are some tips from Mindsinbloom.com to help you start paraphrasing in your meditation time.

1. Reword—Replace words and phrases with synonyms whenever you can.
2. Rearrange—Rearrange words within sentences to make new sentences. You can even rearrange the ideas presented within the paragraph.
3. Realize—Realize that some words and phrases cannot be changed—names, dates, titles, etc., cannot be replaced, but you can present them differently in your paraphrase.
4. Recheck—Make sure that your paraphrase conveys the same meaning as the original text.[10]

## Listen to a Meditation App

In mid-March 2020, the world as we knew it came to an abrupt halt. Restaurants closed, church doors were locked, and all the major news networks talked about the pandemic 24/7. We all experienced different emotions and reactions. Sometimes we took our emotions out on those we care about the most. People who I thought were my friends were downright snarky to me because my view on what was going on was completely different than theirs. A simple, and what I thought harmless, comment I made in a group chat resulted in a social media graphic "educating" me on why we needed to stay six feet apart.

Social media was a war zone. The news outlets predicted doom and gloom, and I went into a depression. I was obsessed with obtaining any information on the pandemic that I could. Fits of crying and some not-so-nice words were thrown at my husband. My phone once again became my idol, until one day, the Holy Spirit whispered, "Put the phone down!"

I honestly don't remember how I came across the Abide meditation app. All I knew is that I needed something that would take my focus away from Facebook and the news and back toward the Lord.

As quickly as I downloaded the Abide app, I deleted the other apps from my phone that I obsessed over.

It was liberating.

In my opinion, meditating on God's Word is the best form of encouragement when you need to silence the world around you.

My day begins at 5:00 a.m. before my family gets up and texts and emails start. I sit silently in the dark in my favorite chair with my coffee. Through my headphones, the soothing voices of the narrators on the Abide app reading the Word of God comfort my heart and soul. In what I can describe as something only the Lord can do, the topics of the meditations are exactly what I need to hear to begin my day.

I also use this app to listen to soothing sounds throughout the day. This brings me peace and calms my anxiety as the world unravels around me.

At night I use it to listen to a sleep devotional. I have never made it through the whole devotional because within ten minutes I am in a deep sleep.

Another great app is Pause by John Eldredge. This app lets you set a reminder time for a one- three- five- or ten-minute pause time throughout your day. My times are set for 9:15 a.m. and 3:15 p.m. By stopping what I am doing and meditating on what is being spoken from God's Word, I am refreshed and reenergized.

Which meditation method do you want to try? I encourage you to try at least one and go from there. You will be amazed by how the Lord works through meditation!

# CHAPTER 16

## THE SPIRITUAL HABIT OF STUDY

*Your word is a lamp to my feet*
*and a light to my path.*
Psalm 119:105

A few weeks ago, we had a major catastrophe occur in our house. Our Keurig broke.

In bewilderment and panic, my son and I tried to figure out what to do. We need our coffee! Seriously, we cannot function without our coffee!

That sounds a tad dramatic, doesn't it?

In reality, we can live without coffee. If we miss our daily intake, what is the worst that will happen? We get a headache and become unbearable to those around us, but it's not the end of the world. As usual, the Lord used this situation as a learning experience and confirmed the nudges of truth He had been feeding me for the past few weeks. "You think you need coffee to get through the day; what you need is more of the Word."

### We Have Immediate Access to the Bible

I sometimes struggle with where to begin when reading the Bible on my own. Yes, I do my daily Bible study and read the required verses but sitting down on my own, without a guided study, is hard for me. I've got the time and the resources, and the pushing of the Holy Spirit (note, I said pushing and not nudging!), so why is it hard for me to sit and actually read the Word?

In *Spiritual Disciplines for the Christian Life*, Donald Whitney describes a time on a mission trip when he and his team encountered a church eager to learn more of the Word. No one, not the minister, the deacons, nor anyone in the congregation had a Bible. The minister would preach a few sermons that he had heard from memory. Whitney and his team pooled their money to buy inexpensive Bibles for the congregation.

Whitney writes, "Most of us shake our heads in pity at such sad conditions. Fact is, however, that many of us have more Bibles in our homes than entire churches have in some impoverished or isolated parts of the world. *But it's one thing to be unfamiliar with Scripture when you don't own a Bible, it's another when you have a bookshelf full.*"[11] (emphasis added)

Ouch.

Double ouch.

One glance at my bookshelf reveals numerous Bibles in various translations, and when I am away from home, I use a Bible app on my phone. I have immediate access to the Word of God, at any given time.

The more we open our Bibles and study the Word, the more we will know God and His forgiveness and unconditional love. Throughout the pages of Scripture, we read the account of the creation of the earth, the beginning and fall of humankind, and the faith and trust of people following God. Woven in the text are God's words of redemption and forgiveness. And in the New Testament we learn of the earthly life and ultimate love and sacrifice of our Savior. From the angels telling Zechariah, Mary, and Joseph of Jesus's birth, to His public ministry of preaching, teaching, and healing and His death and resurrection, the Bible is God's love letter to us.

If we know that this book is the ultimate love letter, why do we open it only on Sundays and not any other day of the week? In a 2017 study by the American Bible Society (ABS), 35.8 percent of Christian women spend time in the Bible weekly, 28.6 percent of women rarely open it, and 23.8 percent never open their Bibles during the week. What a sad statistic.

I mention this statistic because I was the woman who didn't open her Bible between Sundays. Life is busy, and our calendars are full. Maybe we are intimidated by it, or we don't even know where to begin. We don't need to be a theologian to study the Bible; we just need a little time and an open heart and mind.

Whitney states his thoughts bluntly. "The most critical discipline is the intake of God's Word . . . if you want to be changed, if you want to become more like Jesus Christ, discipline yourself to read the Bible."[12]

Reading and studying the Word is crucial to our spiritual transformation. In our growing relationship with Christ, studying Scripture will allow us to fully understand the love the Father has for us. Page after page tells the story of God's loving plan for His children. Are parts of the Bible hard to understand? Yes. Take Leviticus and Numbers, for example. Moses provides the Hebrew people with instructions and laws on how to live according to the Lord's design. It's hard to apply them to our lives today, but remember what Paul says in his second letter to Timothy, "All Scripture is breathed out by God and profitable for teaching, for reproof, for correction, and for training in righteousness" (2 Timothy 3:16). *All* Scripture, not some, is breathed out by God, including those books of the Bible that we feel do not apply to us in this season of our lives.

If you are struggling as I was with self-doubt about reading and comprehending Scripture, please remove those doubts from your mind right now (this is easier said than done!). God's love for you is woven throughout those pages. Every time you open your Bible the Lord is eagerly waiting to meet you with open arms. If you think that you are not good enough due to past sins, please remember that you are forgiven. Think of the Bible as a well of fresh water refilling your soul every day.

## Preparing and Praying to Dig Deeper

There are many ways to study Scripture, and I think I've tried every single one. Here's what I've learned. I'm not studying to be a theologian. I am studying the Word to increase my faith and to grow a deeper relationship with Christ. Throughout the years of raising my boys, I've learned that if I just got one verse read during the day, it was still one verse that I was able to get in during my busy day. And I call that a win!

So, what are the best ways to study Scripture? What works for me may not work for you. I suggest that you try a few of the ways I've listed and find the best fit for your current mothering stage. As your children grow older, you can adjust or add to these study methods. These are, by no means, a complete list of methods, but these are the ones that I have used and found effective.

So, grab your favorite beverage, a journal for note-taking, some post-it notes, and put your phone on "do not disturb." Use the journal to write down any questions or observations you may have while reading. I keep the post-it notes handy to jot down something unrelated to my Scripture reading that inevitably pops into my head. A quick note ensures I'll see to it later and does not distract me entirely from my study.

Ask the Lord to give you wisdom and understanding as you study the Word. Incorporate specific Bible verses pertaining to Scripture study, such as Psalm 119:105, "Your word is a lamp to my feet and a light to my path," or Hebrews 4:12, "For the word of God is living and active, sharper than any two-edged sword, piercing to the division of soul and of spirit, of joints and of marrow, and discerning the thoughts and intentions of the heart."

## Some Ways to Study and Read Scripture

Begin with an overview of the passage, starting with the five W's:

1. Who: Who wrote the book and who is the audience?
2. What: What is it about? What event is taking place? What is the purpose of the book?
3. When: When was this written?

4. Where: Where did the events or happenings take place?

5. Why: Why was it written?

By answering these questions, you will have a better understanding of the chapter's background and context.

## Bold to Bold

When I started reading the Bible, I was pregnant and tired. My mind could only comprehend a few verses at a time, yet I was determined to get as much reading done as possible. I decided to read from subheading to subheading. Look for the bold subheadings in your Bible. By focusing on these short chunks of text, I stayed engaged in the Word without being overwhelmed. The amount of text you read each time using this method can vary, as the number of verses between subheadings varies.

For example, John 4 in the Christian Standard Version lists the subheadings as Jesus and the Samaritan Woman and The Ripened Harvest. Between those two bold subheadings are twenty-five verses, a manageable read.

## Write Out the Chapter

It's a proven fact that if you write out something, you will remember what you have written.[13] Why not try this with the chapters of the Bible? Each day write a few verses in your own handwriting until you complete the passage. It doesn't have to be your best penmanship or even in the same color of ink—that doesn't matter. What matters is that you are spending time in the Word.

## Outline It

After reading your selected verses for the day, create an outline highlighting what stood out to you. Use however many sentences you need to remember what you have read using your own words.

## Listen to It

Some days you may not have the time to sit down and devote to the Word. In those moments, grab your phone, and download a Bible app. Many apps include an audio option. You can listen to a passage of Scripture on the way to work or when chauffeuring children to school and after-school activities. The bonus is that if your children are in the car with you, they will be enriched by hearing the Bible also!

## Topical Study

If you want to dive deeper into your Bible, you can do a topical study. A topical study is simple: You choose a topic to study. For example, you want to know what the Bible says about love. Using your concordance in the back of your Bible, you can see how many times the word love is used and the specific Scripture references. This isn't a comprehensive list, though. If you are eager to get a complete list, you can invest in a Bible concordance such as *Strong's Exhaustive Concordance of the Bible*. While using this study method gets you into Scripture, be sure to read the verses before and after the one you are studying. This will give you a better understanding of the context and meaning.

## Inductive Study

If you would really like to dig deeper—and I mean deeper—you can use the inductive study method. This method involves marking and underlining key phrases and words that appear throughout the text. Using different colors of ink pens or pencils you can create your own system of highlighting and markups to remember what you are reading.

## *Lectio Divina*

I first heard of this spiritual discipline practice at my first retreat. *Lectio Divina* means "divine reading." Barton writes in *Sacred Rhythms* that this spiritual practice is "an approach to the Scriptures that sets us up to listen for the word of God to us is in the present moment."[14] Being silent before diving into the Word will clear our minds and help us listen to what the Lord is saying through His Word. With *lectio divina*, you only want to concentrate on a few verses at a time. This is a somewhat time consuming but rewarding spiritual practice. This also takes a great deal of practice. You need to completely shut your mind down and focus solely on God in the quietness that surrounds you.

As you begin reading the verses, you will want to pay attention to any words you feel stirring in your mind or a word that the Lord is laying on your heart. After reading the verse, relax your mind in the quietness. Repeat this step a few more times and write down what the Lord reveals to you. This practice is best used when everyone is out of the house or at a silence and solitude retreat. For more information about creating your own silence and solitude retreat, be sure and read chapter 18. This chapter will give you a step-by-step guide on getting the most out of your sacred experience.

Now that we've talked about various study methods, which one would you like to try?

# CHAPTER 17

## THE SPIRITUAL HABIT OF JOURNALING

*My heart overflows with a pleasing theme;*
*I address my verses to the king;*
*my tongue is like the pen of a ready scribe.*
Psalm 45:1

I've journaled for as long as I can remember. Notebooks and specially designated pens or pencils filled my childhood bedroom. In those days, journaling was more like a diary, reflecting who I liked—my favorite music artists. It was the 1980s, so a lot of my journaling centered around music and friends.

Now, in my late 40s, it is centered around my faith. Journaling requires that I slow down and reflect over the day or events in my life. In this way, I reflect on how and where I see the Lord at work. My journal includes prayer requests for myself, my family, and others as well as the answers to those prayers. Praise and thanksgiving are recorded throughout the pages, as I see how gracious our loving Father is.

In *Habits of Grace*, David Mathis writes, "Journaling is a way of slowing down life for just a few moments and trying to process at least a sliver of it for the glory of God, our own growth and development, and our enjoyment of the details."[15]

## Journaling: Tracking Your Spiritual Growth

While journaling is not specifically mentioned in the Bible, many influential followers of Christ have kept a journal. These treasures are often published, so we can see how the Lord worked in the lives of believers like Jonathan Edwards and missionaries Jim and Elisabeth Elliot.

The spiritual habit of journaling is not to bring glory upon ourselves but to bring glory to God for His work in and through us. It's an effective way to assess aspects of our walk with Christ that need improvement or identify areas the Spirit may be at work in us. Acknowledging these areas need not make us feel guilty, but it may reveal where we need to stay on (or return to) the path to spiritual transformation.

Journaling is a record of your faith journey. In essence, you are preserving your spiritual history. Can you imagine how our grandchildren or great-grandchildren will react when they read our thoughts on Scripture, our prayers, and how the Lord worked through us? Perhaps they are struggling in their faith, and your words could bring them to the feet of Christ and influence them to accept Him as their Lord and Savior.

## Pen and Paper vs. Computer

There is no right or wrong way to journal. You can write as little or as much as you want. You can skip a day or two and then jump right back into it.

There is also no right or wrong method for journaling. You can use your computer, an app, or pen and paper. I'm old-fashioned and prefer to use pen and paper—for two reasons. First, my journaling time is usually early in the morning before my family wakes up. Sitting on my comfortable couch with my Bible, a pen, paper, and coffee, I am solely focusing on the quietness and the words that I am writing and reading. Second, as a writer and a blogger, I am on my computer daily. I need a break from the clicking of the keyboard and the glow of the monitor.

In addition, digital files may not survive for future generations due to changes in format and programming.

Since the onset of the digital age, many of us store our photos and writings on our devices. If the cloud evaporates, future generations will never know what we look like. Physical photos are a thing of the past, and while it's nice to have the capability of storing thousands of images on our phones, they do not cover our walls with the smiles of our loved ones. The same applies to our words. Everyone knows what Times New Roman size 12-point font looks like, but they don't know what grandma's cursive handwriting looks like.

However, if you are more comfortable journaling digitally, then go for it! There are many options for digital journaling. Many women create a simple password-protected blog. In this way, you can share whatever is on your heart—your thoughts, prayers, anguish, and your questions to God—all can be in the form of a blog, but no one will see.

If you have Apple devices, you can create a special folder in the Notes app and begin journaling. For Android users, my friend Jackie recommends the Color Note app. You can use these apps while waiting in the school pickup line or even sitting in a waiting room. Anytime the Lord prompts you to write, you have your journal at your fingertips. Remember to focus just on journaling and resist the temptation to check social media or Pinterest during your journaling time.

## How I Use Journaling

I was in the habit of journaling daily until the day I sensed that I just needed to sit in silence and rest in Jesus. Now, I find myself journaling four or five days a week and sitting in silence and prayer on the other days. Most mornings, the Holy Spirit guides me on what to do. Usually, after a day of studying and writing, my soul wants some quietness, and that's when I am still.

On the days I journal, here are some of the things I notate:

- Date, time, and weather forecast. Recording the weather began when we were experiencing a negative degree morning, and it was more to record my grumbling than anything else.
- Something I am grateful or thankful for. I don't go immediately into my prayer requests because I want to give God thanks for something that He has done in my life.
- A passage of Scripture that either spoke to me or I want to study more. For study, I primarily use the English Standard Version, but I often pull a different version from the bookshelf for a new translator's perspective on a verse, especially if it's one that I've memorized and am more familiar with.
- A confession of sin or an issue that needs to be addressed. Often I pour out in writing something that I've done or said for which I need to seek forgiveness.
- Prayers for myself, my family, and others. Sometimes I only write the name of those who I need to pray for and silently pray for them, or I will write out the whole prayer.
- Answers to prayers. Remember, He answers all our prayers, even if it's not the results we were hoping for!
- Lyrics to a worship song that had an impact on me.
- Bible verses related to my Word of the Year. For 2021, my word is *abide*, and I will use a concordance to dig further into the Word to find verses relating to that specific word.
- My fears. By writing them out, I feel as if I am handing them over to the Lord. They are out of my heart and into His hands.
- Any current events that I want to pray over and let future generations know my thoughts and how they affected me. My journals for 2020 were mostly about the quarantine and the pandemic. Apologies in advance for anyone who stumbles across my journal. It was a very rough year!

## Journaling Can Incorporate Other Spiritual Habits

I often re-read my journals. Some parts are cringe-worthy, but I am happy that I've written them because in looking back I see how the Lord worked through me and my family, and the results grew my relationship with Jesus more.

If you need some journal prompts, here are a few to get you started. When you begin to journal, the words may come slow or haltingly, but they build up and pour out like a waterfall after time.

Journal Prompts:

- My testimony and what lead me to Christ.
- What brings me the most joy in my life?
- What are my strengths and why?
- What are my weaknesses and why?
- Who inspires me the most?
- Write a letter to my future self explaining what the Lord has done in my life.
- Seven things the Lord has given me to share with others.
- What is my current challenge, and what do I need to do to hand it over to the Lord?
- What is one event or situation that shaped my life?
- What are my three most important goals for the year?

## Bible Journaling—Creative and Fun

Remember when stamping and scrapbooking were all the rage, almost twenty years ago? Creative Memories, Stampin' Up, and Close to My Heart home parties filled our calendars and brought women together for the evening. Several scrapbook stores opened and hosted "cropping" weekends. We packed up all our supplies and sat around the tables, laughing and creating scrapbook pages and homemade cards. Well, that's what we'd hoped to do. More than likely, we laughed, ate, and bought more supplies. Later, we'd drag all our materials back home and boast about the one scrapbook page or card that we finished in a three-day weekend.

Life got hectic and digital scrapbooking replaced our hardcopies. Most of my supplies have been packed and put away in a closet. However, a few years ago, a new and creative way to journal made its debut.

Bible journaling offered a way for us to be creative, study the Word, and journal simultaneously. On a rainy weekend, I love to pull out my supplies, put on some praise and worship music, and sit at my desk and create.

You don't need to be artistic to be a Bible journaler. Simply focus on the Word and, if prompted, design something with stamps or stickers. There are even special journaling Bibles with thicker paper than the standard Bibles and wide margins to write your thoughts, prayers, and praise in. If you don't want to go through the hassle of creating something from scratch, many Bibles, such as the Inspired Bible, have images throughout its pages for coloring and painting.

## Journaling Sermon Notes

I also use a journaling Bible for sermon notes. Instead of taking my regular study Bible to church, the journaling Bible is perfect for highlighting the verses of the sermon and note-taking. Our church has a "fill-in-the-blank" section on the church app to take notes on the bullet points listed throughout the sermon. I find this comes in handy when I need to reflect on a sermon later. I don't have to worry about losing the bulletin because my notes are in my Bible's journaling section.

Some of you maybe be cringing over the fact that I write or create art in my Bible. I did too, at first. The Bible is God's sacred words. However, I view this as a process of spiritual transformation. It enables me to reflect on the ways I'm growing in the Word. Each entry is a reminder of what I was doing or what I was studying at a particular point in my life.

As you learn more about the spiritual habit of journaling, I pray that you can reflect on how the Lord worked in your life—last month or five years ago. Remember, we see only a pixel of the image; the Lord sees the whole image.

# CHAPTER 18

## THE SPIRITUAL HABIT
## OF SILENCE AND SOLITUDE

*And rising very early in the morning,*
*while it was still dark, he departed*
*and went out to a desolate place,*
*and there he prayed.*
Mark 1:35

Peanut butter and jelly.
Macaroni and cheese.
Cheeseburgers and fries.
Silence and Solitude.

What do these all have in common? Aside from the fact that I love each of these, they go together. Where there is one, the other is close behind. Yes, you can eat peanut butter by itself, but jelly gives it a little extra sweetness. What good is macaroni without cheese? And when you eat a cheeseburger, you need to have some salty fries with it.

You can't practice the spiritual habit of silence without solitude. Have you ever tried to quiet your heart and listen to the Holy Spirit with the television on, your family milling about, and the dog barking at the neighbors? It doesn't happen, and it won't happen unless you purposefully set aside time for silence and solitude.

Throughout this chapter, I will share some of the ways that I have incorporated daily silence and solitude in my routine. Here's a hint. It involves getting up in the early hours of the morning, or a quiet drive into work, or spending time away from the house.

I wrote about my first experience at a silence and solitude retreat in chapter 10, and in this chapter, I will give you some ideas on what to do when you schedule your own time of silence and solitude.

## Different Term, Same Concept

Silence and solitude and wilderness journey can be considered the same thing. Both seek to remove oneself from outside distractions and focus on the Lord. And as I mentioned before, it's not something that you grab your friends and go off for the weekend for some girlfriend time. It is possible to go with a group and then go your separate ways when you get to the retreat center, only meeting up for morning and evening meetings to reflect on what occurred throughout each other's day.

Seeking individual silence and solitude is hard. It's one of the spiritual habits we need to purposefully schedule into our already hectic days. It's also one of the spiritual habits that can incorporate other habits: meditation, prayer, journaling, worship, and study.

## Start Slow and Avoid the Awkwardness

"Go big or go home" is often a term we use to tackle a big project or check something off our to-do list. If I am committed to doing something, I usually start big and often get overwhelmed in the process. Ultimately, I get frustrated, feel defeated, and give up. I realize a little too late that I am in over my head. My first journey into this spiritual habit ended in just that way—in frustration because I overextended my expectations of what I thought would happen.

The hum of the fluorescent lights drowned my doubt. Sitting at a table at the end of a long, narrow room, my eyes focused on the gray walls—the same walls that I helped paint. They now looked dreary and lifeless. I felt the same way, scared and ashamed, stressed, and overwhelmed. The thought of gathering my things and leaving sounded better by the minute.

One would think I was in some danger. I wasn't. I was sitting in a Sunday school classroom in the little country church that we attended, participating in a women's silence and solitude night. Looking forward with anticipation to the night, I had made sure to have the perfect journal, writing instrument, my iPod (this was pre-iPhone!), and, of course, my Bible. It was my first time participating in something like this, so I made sure I had all the supplies I needed.

Physically, I was prepared; mentally, I was not.

Preparing my heart and mind for this night caused stress that I was not anticipating. Sitting silently in the room, the overwhelming sense that I was not good enough to be in the presence of the Lord filled my mind. The enemy used my feelings to his advantage; I wanted to give up and go home. I was scared because I had no idea what I was getting into or what I would encounter. I was ashamed to admit that after five years of being a believer, my relationship with Christ was stalled. I stressed over the fact that I had only a limited amount of time to accomplish all that I wanted to do, which included diving deep into the Word and hopefully sensing the presence of the Holy Spirit (my hopes were pretty lofty back then!). I knew that once my heart settled, I would enjoy this unique evening. But something else was affecting me. As a mom of young children, it was the one thing that I craved the most: peace and quiet. There was no one yelling, "Mom!" or the TV blaring *Blue's Clues* or *Dora the Explorer*. No dogs barking. No husband talking on the phone.

It was completely silent. And the silence is what bothered me the most.

As I sat in the cold, metal chair, I desperately wanted to leave. I wasn't strong or even focused enough to be participating in something like this. My fear overshadowed my faith, and I had no idea how to make it through the three hours that lay ahead.

That night proved to me what I needed the most—time specifically set aside to focus solely on my relationship with Christ. The seed was planted to cultivate periods of silence and solitude in my life, but I needed to overcome obstacles and time mismanagement to get to the point where I am today.

And you know what? The silence still bothers me sometimes, even today.

## Why Do We Think We Need Noise in Our Lives?

We are surrounded by noise 24/7. With the internet and social media at our fingertips, we are often bombarded with instant notifications that interrupt us amid our daily tasks. That is why silence and solitude are more critical than ever. We need to purposely tune the world's noise out and intentionally focus on the Lord. In *Celebration of Discipline,* Foster writes, "Every distraction of the body, mind, and spirit must be put to a kind of suspended animation before this deep work of God upon the soul can occur."[16]

We need to enter a time of silence when our phones are on "do not disturb" and distractions are minimal or nonexistent.

But how? How do we tune the world out and focus on the Lord?

We ask for guidance from the Lord and then schedule it.

Sounds crazy, doesn't it? Scheduling a time for silence and solitude is just as important as scheduling your hair color or a girls' night out. If we don't physically schedule it, it will not happen.

## Scheduling Silence and Solitude

If you are still using a paper calendar, block out a time. Better yet, schedule a time in your digital calendar and share it with your family. You can also set your alarm or a reminder on your phone. However, writing a time in your calendar is one thing; entering a time of silence and solitude is an act within itself and complex. You need the willpower, determination, and most importantly, you need to be focused enough that nothing will come between you and your time with God—not your children, grandchildren, or even your husband.

During one of my spiritual formation lectures, our professor spoke about Susanna Wesley, mother of two of the most influential men in modern church history—John and Charles Wesley. Susanna was wife to Samuel and mother to nineteen children, nine of whom died during childhood. Susanna was a strong-willed, God-fearing woman who would put her apron over her head when she prayed and read her Bible, when she needed quiet time with the Lord.

This was a subtle sign to her ten children. "I am having my quiet time with the Lord, please don't bother me." The impact this had on her children is still felt today through the works of her sons John and Charles.

If the Lord is nudging you to begin this spiritual habit, He will provide you with a creative way to make it happen!

## Jesus Himself Made Time for Silence and Solitude

With His ministry in full swing, Jesus was teaching, preaching, healing the sick, and raising the dead. If I think my calendar is full, it's nothing compared to what Jesus was doing.

The gospel of Mark tucks a simple but powerful verse in between the healing of many people and preaching. "And rising very early in the morning, while it was still dark, he departed and went out to a desolate place, and there he prayed" (Mark 1:35).

Note, Scripture says *while it was still dark*.

Jesus, who took on human form to save us from our sins, knew what it felt like to be exhausted. Matthew writes that Jesus and His disciples traveled throughout the region of Galilee, teaching in the synagogues and proclaiming the gospel of the kingdom of God. By this time, Jesus had quite the following, and large crowds gathered around them everywhere they went.

We know what that feels like at times, right?

When our children were toddlers, they would follow us all around the house. They were under our feet when we tried to make dinner, and when we tried to have a moment of peace in the bathroom, they were right there waiting for us to come out. I can remember growling and grumbling most of the time! I look back now and realize that I was the center of my boys' world. By following me around the house, they kept close to me because I was the center of their lives.

Jesus was the center of the Jewish people's lives.

This humble servant, son of a carpenter, went throughout the land, healing the people from sickness and diseases. He cast out demons and healed paralytics. Jesus cured all those who came to Him in need of healing.

In the midst of His busy, growing ministry, our Savior made it a priority to set aside time to pray. If our Savior made it a priority for quiet time with the Father, then what excuse do I have not to have quiet time with Him?

If you feel the prompting of the Holy Spirit nudging you to get up early before the rest of your family rises for the day, here are some tips to get started.

## Finding Silence and Solitude Early in the Morning

Soon after the life-changing moment in the middle school parking lot I sensed the Holy Spirit pushing me out of my comfort zone. I came to understand that to have a transformed life I needed to change my daily routine.

At the time I had two school-age children at home. From sunrise to well after dark, I was one hundred percent focused on my children— from getting them out the door for school to volunteering at school, to sports and activities after school, to the endless amount of homework, to finally falling into bed for a few hours of sleep. The same routine held fast day after day. I was still committed to reading my Bible while waiting for the boys to get out of school, so what more could I give Him?

More time, that's what.

But when could I possibly devote more time to God?

"Wake up earlier!" the Holy Spirit whispered to me.

"No!" was my answer straight back to Him.

I'm not a morning person. Never have been and never will be. So, when the Lord laid on my heart to set aside a time of silence and solitude, I panicked and tried to come up with every excuse imaginable not to.

"Get up and spend some quiet time with Me!"

What? I barely got enough sleep as it was, and the Lord was prompting me to wake up even earlier? That couldn't be the only option that I had.

What proceeded in the following days was an argument with the Lord—Who, by the way, always wins! I finally gave in and set my alarm thirty minutes earlier than usual. The Lord shoves those He loves, and He shoved me right out of the comfort of my nice, warm bed.

On the first morning of my new routine, I woke up fifteen minutes before my alarm went off. Wide awake and without the urge to hit the snooze button, the Lord had won the battle over His strong-willed daughter, who wasn't and still isn't a morning person. I thank God every day for creating coffee. I like to think that when He created it, He made it especially for me because it would take this delightful beverage and a shove from above to get me awake and in the mindset of silence and solitude.

## You've Committed to Getting Up Early—Now What?

I set the alarm for thirty minutes ahead of my usual wake-up time because my family would not be up yet, and the house was quiet. Once everyone wakes up, your focus will be on them and not your quiet time.

Set the alarm for a manageable time. As your body and mind adjust to getting up earlier than usual, you can gradually increase your time. My alarm is now set for 4:45 a.m. so that I can have a good hour with the Lord.

Indulge in your favorite morning wake-me-up beverage. Thank you, Lord, for coffee! Grab your Bible and journal, and feel free to sit in your favorite chair with a cozy blanket. Don't get too comfy, though! You may fall back asleep—trust me on this because I speak from experience! If you have your phone with you, be sure to silence it.

If you feel inclined to do so, put on some praise and worship music. I find Pandora's "Instrumental Christian Songs" station to be a great addition to my silence and solitude time. Recently, I incorporated the Abide app into my morning routine. The soothing sounds of a stream running in the background keep my mind focused on the Lord. On the mornings when I feel prompted to just sit in silence, I sit in an upright, relaxed position and try to focus on the Lord without having the upcoming events of my day creep in.

After getting situated, proceed to sit in silence for the first few minutes. If you are anything like me, something unrelated to prayer will creep into your mind—for example, an item you need to pick up at the grocery store or something you need to tell your child before leaving for school. Keep a notebook nearby, jot that thought down on a piece of paper, and continue with your silence and solitude time. You will find it easy to get back into your quiet time once it's written down and out of the way.

## Finding Silence and Solitude in Walks

Every morning at 6:30 a.m., I see her walking. Standing in my front yard, in sweats or pajamas, I nod at her and whisper, "Good morning." She waves back and continues walking, reading the devotional prayer book that she covets in her hands.

My sweet neighbor power walks and takes time for silence and solitude at the same time. While she's walking past us, I'm getting glared at by an elderly cocker spaniel who is none too happy that I woke him up from a peaceful slumber to do his morning business. We are clearly in two different worlds when we see each other in the morning.

This is just one example of making time for silence and solitude. My neighbor's idea of combining those two things in the early morning hours is brilliant! Not only is she getting some exercise, but she is also taking in God's creation. Whether in sub-freezing temperatures or in the heat and humidity, she's walking with her devotional in hand and her lips moving as she softly prays.

## Finding Silence and Solitude while Driving

Another way to be creative in your silence and solitude time is driving. If you are alone in the car, turn the radio off and just sit in silence. Listen for the Lord's whispers or let Him know what's on your mind. Have a conversation with Him. He's there, and He's listening. It's hard to drive and pray with your eyes closed, so keep them open and enjoy your time alone with Him.

## Going the Distance—Twenty-Four-Hour or Forty-Eight-Hour Silence and Solitude Retreats

That first silence and solitude retreat at the Christian camp all those years ago set a precedent, and I have since tried to attend three or four a year. While it's possible to have an excellent personal retreat at home, I find that there are too many distractions. I have much better results when I leave the comforts of my own home and travel to a specific place.

There are two different retreats I have participated in—ones led by others and ones self-lead. A neighboring town was home to a wonderful Catholic retreat center. Set in a rural area, the center provided a private room with a bath and meals for a reasonable rate. Sadly, when the pandemic hit, the center fell victim to the economic failures of the time and closed permanently. I cried when I saw the post on Facebook.

Silence and solitude is an ancient practice recognized by Christians throughout the ages. As I am writing this, I am in desperate need of a personal retreat. My soul thirsts for it. Fourteenth-century mystic St. John of the Cross refers to this as "the dark night of the soul." When we think of the term dark, we assume it is terrible. While it is a difficult experience, it can be compared to a surgery to heal someone from a sickness. My soul is sick. The stress of living during a pandemic, the grief over the deaths of my brother and dad, and transitioning from raising children to an empty nester have weighed heavily on me.

"The dark night is one of the ways God brings us into a hush, a stillness so that he may work an inner transformation upon the soul,"[17] writes Foster. I need a hush and stillness. I am currently searching for a retreat center, but in the meantime, I still participate in my daily silence and solitude in the mornings.

## Ways to Refresh Your Soul During a Retreat

You have cleared your calendar and booked a twenty-four-hour silence and solitude stay at a retreat center. Now what?

Here are some tips to get you started:

1. In the days leading up to your retreat, be in prayer. Ask the Lord for guidance and direction on preparing your heart for what lies ahead. Pray through the whole armor of God (Ephesians 6:10-18), because the enemy isn't going to like that you are devoting time to the Lord. There will be spiritual warfare going on during your silence and solitude time, and it's best to "armor up" and stand firm in the Lord, even before you set foot in the retreat center.

2. What to pack: along with the essentials, you will want to pack your Bible, a journal, pens, Bible study materials, devotionals, and headphones.

3. When you get to the retreat center, take some time to walk the grounds and find your way around. It's hard to set aside the daily rush of life. You will want to ease into your silence and solitude time.

4. Once you've become familiar with your surroundings, begin listening to some praise and worship music. Praising the Lord through worship will get your mind and heart set for the hours to come.

5. Sleep peacefully. You do not have a strict schedule to follow. Sleep in if you need to. Rest is part of soul care, and soul care is part of silence and solitude.

6. After breakfast, begin to pray or read your Bible. Whatever the

Holy Spirit directs you to do, be ready to listen and obey His direction.

7. Throughout your retreat time, journal anything that the Holy Spirit reveals to you. Record your thoughts, feelings, prayer requests, and praise reports.

Letitia Suk wrote a fabulous book on personal retreats. *Getaway with God: the Everywoman's Guide to Personal Retreat* provides you with daily guided instructions to help you make the most of your retreat. It's a wonderful resource for those who may need a little structure during the retreat.

As with any spiritual habit, silence and solitude will lead you on the path of transformation. Finding rest for your weary soul is something that needs to be routinely practiced. Schedule a retreat and see how the Lord works throughout your time with Him!

# CHAPTER 19

$\textit{——}$ ⊙≿⊙ $\textit{——}$

## THE SPIRITUAL HABIT OF FASTING

*And when you fast, do not look gloomy like the hypocrites,*
*for they disfigure their faces that their fasting may be seen by others.*
*Truly, I say to you, they have received their reward.*
*But when you fast, anoint your head and wash your face,*
*that your fasting may not be seen by others*
*but by your Father who is in secret.*
*And your Father who sees in secret will reward you.*
Matthew 6:16–18

*C*an I be honest with you? Prayer, meditation, study, journaling, silence and solitude, and worship are my favorite habits to practice. I struggle with fasting.

Big time.

And since I'm being honest—it's my least favorite. I think it stems from my Catholic upbringing. I attended a Catholic school for eight years, and each Lent we were to write out what we were giving up for the season. And each year, I would write down the food that I didn't enjoy—for example, Brussel sprouts. I would like to state for the record, not one time in my childhood did my aunt ever fix my brother and me Brussel sprouts. So, why did I write down that I was fasting from those unique vegetables? Because one of my classmates told me at recess that they were horrible and to never, ever eat them. Now, I realize I didn't know the true meaning of fasting. I have a better grasp on its purpose now, and I am trying to incorporate it into my spiritual life, but it's hard.

Fasting is a work in progress for me—as are all the spiritual habits: In transforming our lives to Christ's image "from one degree of glory to another" (2 Corinthians 3:18). Changing to be more Christlike doesn't happen overnight, but developing spiritual habits in our lives enables us to slowly, step-by-step become more like Him.

On a side note, as an adult, I love Brussel sprouts roasted in the air fryer with a little bit of garlic powder, sea salt, and olive oil.

I love food.

In fact, I love food a little *too* much. When I first heard of the spiritual habit of fasting, I immediately thought, "That's not one I'm going to partake in!"

Nope. Nada. I am not going to do it. And besides, not eating makes me "hangry." I imagine myself in the middle of a Snickers commercial with me as the main star and my family handing over one of those delicious candy bars to calm me down and cure my hanger.

After many failed attempts to participate in this spiritual habit, here is what I've come to realize, it's not about me. It's not about food. It's about abstaining from food so that I can focus intentionally on God through prayer. It's all about God. Sounds simple, right? It's not as easy as it sounds.

As believers, we are called to fast. Fasting is mentioned in more than seventy verses in both the Old and New Testament. Moses fasted for forty days and forty nights without any food or water when he was on the mountain with God (Exodus 34:28). Elijah ate one meal before traveling for forty days and nights without food or water to Mt. Horeb (1 Kings 19:8). Queen Esther and her cousin, Mordecai, instructed the Jews in Susa and her household to refrain from eating and drinking for three days before she went to her husband, King Ahasuerus, unannounced (Esther 4:15–17). Daniel fasted for three weeks, abstaining from meat and wine, after receiving a terrifying vision (Daniel 10:2–3). Anna, an eighty-four-year-old prophetess, fasted and prayed at the temple day and night until she set her eyes on the infant Messiah (Luke 2:36–38). And Jesus Himself fasted from food for forty days and nights while being tempted by the enemy (Matthew 4:1–11).

With all the mention of fasting in the Word, why is this one of the most challenging spiritual habits to practice? I believe it's because the enemy has fooled us into believing that we are weak and cannot power through a fast. Add in the moment that our stomach starts to growl, our minds go to the images of comfort food. Physical hunger and craving overpower our soul's spiritual hunger.

Usually flesh wins over the spirit. Thankfully, we have a God who is bigger than us and encourages us to power through the inconvenience of a growling stomach and focus on Him.

## Why Fast?

Fasting isn't the subject of a Sunday sermon, and friends generally avoid the topic. That's because fasting is a personal matter. Jesus called out the hypocrites of His day for making a show of their fasting. They purposely looked downcast so their neighbors would notice and perhaps ask why they were so upset or gloomy (Matthew 6:16–18). It's important to note that the Law only required fasting on the Day of Atonement. It was another thing to add to a long list of laws that were cumbersome. The religious leaders attempted to show themselves as being more holy and religious than other people, and Jesus saw them for who they were—fakes.

In an article for the Gospel Coalition, David Kakish wrote, "Fasting is not about creating personal suffering and loss in order to teach ourselves we need God. Fasting is harnessing the pain that'll inevitably come as we try to obey God in a fallen world and leveraging the opportunity to hide in Christ, run to him for strength, and throw ourselves at the foot of his throne."[18]

For me, the best time to fast is when I am facing something that I need to devote to prayer, such as healing for a loved one, grieving over a significant loss, acknowledging my guilt over a sin I committed, or asking for guidance over a significant decision. Anything that requires my undivided attention in prayer is reason to fast.

## Start Small and then Build Up

Unlike the spiritual habits of prayer or study, fasting isn't sponta-neous. Prayerfully plan when and what type of fast to undertake. Start with baby steps. A beginning runner doesn't run a marathon immedi-ately after buying a pair of running shoes. She trains each day, slowly increasing her running time. She will build up to run a 5K, then a 10K, and when she feels comfortable enough, she will run a half marathon. When she feels she has trained long and hard enough, she signs up for the marathon that she always dreamed of running.

The same applies to fasting. God will not call us to a forty-day desert fast as Jesus did at the outset of his ministry. It's important to start slow, so that both your body and mind can prepare for what you encounter. Your mindset must be for God to sustain you, not food. Fasting is God-centered, not self-centered. If I go into a fast with the mentality of fasting from food to lose weight, it's an instant failure. I'm focusing on myself more than God.

Our motive for fasting is not to change God's mind or earn His favor. We fast because, as Donald Whitney states, "Fasting can be a testi-mony—even one directed to yourself—that you find your greatest plea-sure and enjoyment in the life from God."[19]

## Four Types of Fasting

There are several ways to fast. However, if you are sick, pregnant or nursing, have diabetes, gout, cancer, a compromised immune system, or a chronic disease, please do not fast. I'll discuss other means of fast-ing later in the chapter. Consult your doctor if you have any questions about your health prior to fasting.

Also, while it's not normal to announce that you are going into a fast, be sure to let a family member know in case a health situation arises.

Stay hydrated. Juice and water will give you the strength needed to finish your fast. When Jesus fasted in the wilderness, biblical scholars assume it was a regular fast, meaning that He didn't consume food but drank water. Luke writes in his Gospel, "And Jesus, full of the Holy Spirit, returned from the Jordan and was led by the Spirit in the wilderness for forty days, being tempted by the devil. And *he ate nothing* during those days. And when they were ended, *he was hungry*" (Luke 4:1–2 emphasis added).

There are several different types of fast. Here are a few examples:

1.  Regular Fast: Refraining from eating food but maintain liquids such as water and fruit juice.
2.  Partial Fast: Refraining from eating a particular type of food or omitting a meal. In order not to defile himself with King Nebuchadnezzar's food or succumb to the temptations of the Babylonian culture, Daniel and his friends ate only vegetables and drank water (Daniel 1:8–14).
3.  Full Fast: No food or liquid is consumed. This was the type of fast Queen Esther called for before she entered the inner court of the king to save the Jews from death (Esther 4:15–17).
4.  Fast from Worldly Desires: Giving up something that consumes our thoughts and activities that tend to monopolize our time. One example of this would be refraining from social media for a set length of time.

## Pray First, then Fast

Fasting takes planning, and usually it is not an impromptu act. When facing a circumstance beyond our control, fasting invites us to focus entirely on the Lord for strength and guidance.

If you are prompted through prayer to begin a fast, plan ahead. Ask yourself, what kind of fast you'll partake in. Remember, start slow.

Of the examples I listed, the two that I participate in the most are the partial fast and fasting from worldly desires. I break from social media every Friday evening to Sunday afternoon. I would break from it completely; however, most of my Bible studies and writers' groups that I participate in and administer are all on social media.

I've participated in partial fasts when grieving the sudden deaths of my brother and father who passed away within five weeks of each other. When facing a major career decision, writing this book, for example, I fasted to ask guidance from the Lord on whether I should publish or not. This book is the answer to that fast.

My partial fast has consisted of either fasting from a lunch meal or partaking in fruits and vegetables. For me, it's easier to do over the lunch hour because those are the hours I work. The moment my stomach begins to growl, I start praying either a silent or audible prayer—depending on who is in the office with me.

Here are some tips for when the Lord nudges you to fast. Rest assured, He *will* nudge you!

1. Start slow. Determine what is the best fast for you.
2. If you are new to fasting, it's best to fast from one meal and let your body become accustomed to this spiritual habit.
3. Many people fast from breakfast to breakfast or lunch to lunch. By doing this, you are missing only two meals.
4. Keep hydrated. Water or juice are musts, especially if you are new to fasting.
5. Once your fast is over, slowly eat small portions of food. It's not the time to go to the Chinese buffet (trust me on this one!). Let your body adjust to eating again.

As you practice the spiritual habit of fasting, God will be working through you. Focus on what God is doing spiritually and not what your body is doing physically.

As Foster writes, "Fasting can bring breakthroughs in the spiritual realm that will never happen in any other way. It is a means of God's grace and blessing that should not be neglected any longer."[20]

# CHAPTER 20

*THE SPIRITUAL HABIT OF WORSHIP*

> *But when he saw the wind, he was afraid,*
> *and beginning to sink he cried out, "Lord, save me."*
> *Jesus immediately reached out his hand and took hold of him,*
> *saying to him, "O you of little faith, why did you doubt?"*
> *And when they got into the boat, the wind ceased.*
> *And those in the boat worshiped him, saying,*
> *"Truly you are the Son of God."*
> Matthew 14:30–34

*I*t had been almost a year since we walked through the doors. Fifty-one weeks, to be exact. The smell of the cedar in the entryway reminded me of a time when life was normal. Living in only one of the three states where restrictions regarding the pandemic were stricter than the rest of the United States, churches in Illinois opened later than any other Midwestern state. Capacity was capped at a certain percentage of members, sign-ups were required, and temperatures were checked at the door. To be honest, it wasn't worth the hassle to go. It was easier watching the online service from the comforts of our couch rather than making the effort to attend in-person worship.

But we were missing out on corporate worship, and it was affecting us significantly. At times my soul thirsted for that type of worship, and we discussed going back to in-person services, but we came up with some excuses and then more excuses. It was comfortable to stay home. There was no frantic race to get to church on time. There wasn't a mom yelling, "It's time to go. Get in the car now!" Or "You aren't wearing that to church. Go change!" In fact, on many Sundays, I was late getting to the couch for the 9:00 a.m. service. We enjoyed our lazy Sunday mornings, relaxing in our sweats or pajamas. The enemy thrived at seeing us not attend a physical service because our hearts weren't entirely into it. My sons would roll out of bed at 8:55 a.m., plop down on the couch, and either drift back to sleep or eat breakfast. We tried to sing the worship songs, but again, we just didn't put much effort into it.

The enemy was winning this battle. He loved that our hearts weren't into the service. He loved that praise and worship were nonexistent from our hearts and lips.

Enemy - 1, Eversoles - 0

Today the enemy lost. The Eversoles were back in church.

Eversoles - 1, Enemy - 0

## Making a Joyful Noise

Oh, how my heart sang as we walked through those church doors today! Guilt overcame me as I realized we should have done this sooner. Compromised immune systems and physical limitations are legitimate reasons for not attending in-person services; however, these factors didn't apply to us. We were physically able; we just didn't want to move from our comfortable positions on the couch.

One of the positive things that came out of the pandemic was how churches could livestream their services. Almost instantly, churches adapted to the new, hopefully temporary, way of serving their people—even to people who have never walked through the doors of the church. The pastor continued preaching, and the praise and worship team kept the music going despite not having anyone in the pews.

The church adjusted and continued in one of the most tumultuous years most of us have ever experienced. Missing out on a Sunday worship service meant my family and I were missing out on the spiritual habit of worship, and that's not good. We were made to worship the Lord, and by not doing it, we miss the connection and adoration that God deserves.

## What is Worship?

Donald Whitney describes worship like this: "to worship God means to ascribe the proper worth to God, to magnify His worthiness of praise, or better to approach and address God as He is worthy."[21]

Worship in the spiritual habit form is adoration and reverence for God. Devotion, glorify, exalt, magnify, praise, thanksgiving, exaltation, and honor are just some of the words used to describe worship. Worship can also have a negative connotation when we worship something that becomes an idol to us.

Who is God to you? Pause for a second and think about that. *Who is God to you?* Which one of those words, describes your thoughts on worship? For many of us, the word *worship* brings to mind praise songs sung during church. Worship is that. However, it's so much more. It's putting God before ourselves, our families, our jobs, and our friends. It's a daily expression of love and gratitude toward the One who loves us so much that He sent His one and only Son to redeem us from our sins.

Whitney describes this perfectly when he writes, "the more we focus on God, the more we understand and appreciate His infinite worth."[22] God is good, and He is worthy of our praise!

## Worship—From the Old Testament to the New Testament, Praise God!

A quick search for the word *worship* on Biblegateway.com resulted in over 180 verses from Genesis to Revelation and from Abraham to the Apostles which speak of worship.

In the Old Testament, Abraham worshiped the Lord before placing Isaac on the altar (Genesis 22:5). Isaac bowed his head in worship after he met Rebekah (Genesis 24:26). As the Hebrew people were preparing for the final plague, the death of the firstborn, and the first Passover, the people bowed in worship (Exodus 4:31). When Joshua confronted a commander of the army of the Lord, he "fell on his face to the earth and worshiped him," (Joshua 5:14). After David and Bathsheba's child died, David washed and anointed himself, changed his clothes, and went to the "house of the LORD and worshiped" (2 Samuel 12:20). Nehemiah writes how the people of Israel came together to confess their sins and remember all the Lord had done for them, professing, "the host of heaven worships you" (Nehemiah 9:6). After losing his family and property and having his friends turn on him, Job still worshiped the Lord (Job 1:20).

Worship doesn't end in the Old Testament. Forty days after His birth, Mary and Joseph presented Jesus at the temple and encountered Anna, the prophetess. Widowed after only seven years of marriage, she dedicated her life wholly to the Lord. She would not depart from the temple. For years, Anna fasted, prayed, and worshiped until at the age of 84, her eyes set upon the Redeemer, Himself (Luke 2:37). The wise men "fell down and worshiped" the toddler Jesus (Matthew 2:11). In speaking to the woman at the well, Jesus informed her that "those who worship him (God) must worship in spirit and truth" (John 4:24). After healing the blind man, Jesus asked him a simple but important question. "Do you believe in the Son of Man?" His reply? "Lord, I believe," and he worshiped Him (John 9:35, 38). After Jesus's ascension into heaven, his followers worshiped Him (Luke 24:52).

The book of Revelation alone has twenty-two verses dedicated to worship. Twenty-four elders fell down before God in worship (Revelation 4:10), the angels surround the throne and worship (Revelation 7:11), and the angel reminds John to worship God and God alone (Revelation 22:9).

Worship God. Those two words are not only powerful, but they are a command. To say that worship isn't important in our spiritual transformation is an understatement. True worship is sincere and from the heart. If it's not, it's not authentic worship.

## Idol Worship

There is another form of worship, and that is idol worship. In our culture many things other than God, compete for our attention. Idol worship is as prevalent today as it was in the Old Testament—our idols only look different. The Old Testament records numerous instances of idol worship, from the Israelites worshiping the golden calf to worshiping the gods of their enemies. In the New Testament, Paul addresses the men of Athens about their idol worship—my favorite is when he calls them out for worshiping an altar of an "unknown god" (Acts 17:23). Today, our idols may be our phones, sports teams, Netflix, pornography, food, and whatever else is getting our undivided attention. Our fixations topple our worship of the Lord.

## Corporate Worship

In our first in-person service following the pandemic hiatus, tears formed in my eyes as we sang the first worship song. A multitude of voices coming together and praising the Lord filled my soul and refreshed my dry bones. I noticed people around me lifting their hands in praise.

How can we not worship the Lord with all our hearts in a church service? When we get caught up in our surroundings and the people, that's how. Maybe it's the worship leader who you think is showing off a little too much. Or perhaps you cannot figure out why that woman wore what she did? Full disclosure, I've thought these things and more. I can get caught up in the external side of the church and completely miss the opportunity to worship the Lord fully. The Holy Spirit has taught me that when I see the worship leader praising the Lord, I'm not to be judgmental. He may be genuinely in the moment and worshiping the Lord. And that woman wearing an outfit that I don't particularly care for? Well, I'm sure I've worn some mismatched articles of clothing before, and people probably thought the same thing about me. It's not my job to judge. It is my job, however, to pray those I fellowship with.

That's what I love about a church service. From the moment we walk through the doors until we say goodbye to the greeter as we leave the building, we are in worship. As church members, we can all come together and, with one common goal, worship the Lord through fellowship, song, and prayer.

## Personal Worship

Corporate worship on Sundays is not the end of worship for us. We must continue to worship throughout the week. By participating in other spiritual habits, such as prayer, study, mediation, and even journaling, we focus on the Lord and worship Him on our own. I love how the spiritual habits blend in a common goal—to be more like Christ.

Amid the chaos of the busyness of our lives, carving time out for worship brings joy to the Lord. We are connected to Him, and like a proud Father, He cherishes our time together.

Worship can take place anytime or anywhere.

## In the Car, Home, and at Your Job—Worship Him!

When you feel the pressing of the Holy Spirit telling you to slow down and focus on God for a few minutes, don't ignore it! No matter how busy you are, turning on some uplifting music will lift your spirits. Thanks to our phones, we have access to Christian music artists at all times.

Need some good-feeling, beat-thumping music? TobyMac and Mandisa work for me.

Or maybe your day is just not going well at all. The house is a mess, the washer broke, and you just don't have the funds to fix it. In despair, quiet your heart, say a prayer, and listen to some praise and worship music.

I love how the Lord always provides the exact song I need to lift my heart and soul. I have the local radio station streaming in the background while I work in the kitchen, and I am amazed at the song lyrics that I hear. When you stop and focus on them, they are prayers set to music. They will bring tears to your eyes, and soon you will be singing along with them.

I don't listen to praise and worship 24/7 because I'm an 80s girl, and listening to my childhood songs brings back memories of growing up in a different time and era. However, when that whisper from the Holy Spirit nudges me to turn the channel or change the artist on my phone, I do because I know that the Lord is about to do something powerful. It's time to pay attention and focus.

As we go about our days, let's take a moment and worship the One who loves us. Let's set aside time to listen to some music or take a walk and admire the beauty that surrounds us. Let's drown out what the outside world is throwing at us and reach for the One who will calm our fears and love us unconditionally.

# CHAPTER 21

## BIBLICAL REFLECTION—HANNAH, MOTHER OF SAMUEL AND PRAYER WARRIOR

*And Hannah prayed and said,*
*"My heart exults in the LORD; my horn is exalted in the LORD.*
*My mouth derides my enemies, because I rejoice in your salvation.*
*There is none holy like the LORD: for there is none besides you;*
*there is no rock like our God."*
1 Samuel 2:1–2

*D*edicated, faithful, and obedient to the Lord; these are just a few words that describe mothers we meet in the Bible. These women were ordinary, everyday women who would become mothers of kings, prophets, leaders, and even the Messiah—the Savior of the world.

Faithful followers of the Lord, these mothers not only put their complete trust in Him, but each also had a consistent prayer life.

In biblical times women were considered possessions. Though subservient to her husband, a wife held an esteemed position in the household. A wife's central role was to produce a family, particularly sons, who would continue the family name. Women were in charge of the daily household chores, raising their children, and teaching basic life lessons. Around the age of six, the sons would head off to work with their fathers, while the daughters stayed at home and learned about weaving, cooking, and other skills to prepare them for the time they married.

The role of the wife and mother would evolve throughout biblical times, and her role would be held in high esteem, as described in Proverbs 31. Jesus Himself viewed women with the utmost importance. From revealing who He was to the Samaritan woman at the beginning of His ministry, to dining with Mary and Martha, to appearing to Mary Magdalene after His resurrection, women were a pivotal part of Jesus's ministry.

One of my favorite biblical mothers is Hannah, the mother of the prophet Samuel.

Her story can be found in 1 Samuel 1–2:21.

## Hannah

"I wonder what will happen today?" Hannah thought as she adjusted her eyes to the morning light. Lying in bed, she dreaded the thought of getting up and facing Peninnah, her husband's other wife.

Barren, Hannah faced daily ridicule from Peninnah. Although Peninnah gave birth to numerous sons and daughters, Elkanah loved Hannah more, which made her the object of Peninnah's jealous behavior. Hannah endured the heartbreak of infertility as well Peninnah's scorn. She longed for a child.

Today they would travel to the temple for the yearly sacrifice to the LORD of hosts at Shiloh. As Hannah slowly made her way out of the tent, she immediately felt the glare of Peninnah.

"It's going to be a bad day," she muttered to herself. Sure, Elkanah would give her double portions of the sacrifice, but that would only fuel the fire of the hateful, spiteful words from Peninnah.

Peninnah had it all—with one exception. She was socially accepted, a wife and a mother. But the one thing that she lacked was the love of her husband. She saw daily how much more attention Hannah received from Elkanah. In her jealousy, she did what many women would do—she used hateful words to destroy a human spirit.

"You may have Elkanah's heart, but I have his children," Peninnah said repeatedly. With each word, the pain in Hannah's heart increased to the point where the grief and anguish took over her life. The heartache was so severe that Hannah could not eat. Her physical and mental health started to decline.

Her incessant weeping and refusal to eat troubled her poor husband. Confused, as most husbands are when it comes to their wives' emotions, Elkanah didn't get the real reason why Hannah was so sorrowful.

"Hannah, why aren't you eating? And why are you crying so much? Do I not mean more to you than ten sons?" Elkanah said to her after she refused the double portion that he offered to her.

Bless his heart. While Elkanah had concern and love for Hannah, he still didn't completely understand Hannah's yearning for a child.

Realizing that she couldn't go on like this any longer, Hannah turned to the one person who would know her most inner thoughts and desires. The one person who had been by her side throughout her entire life.

"I will go to the LORD," Hannah thought. "He sees my pain and suffering and He will comfort me."

With what little strength and courage Hannah had, she got up, dusted off her clothes, and walked to the house of the Lord. When she arrived, she openly wept as she prayed to God for a son.

"Oh, LORD, would You look on your servant with compassion and remember me in these times?" she prayed to the Lord. "If You give me a son, I will give him back to You all the days of his life."

She felt Eli the priest staring and didn't care what others thought about her bold act of faith. Eli thought she was drunk because he saw Hannah's lips move, but no sound came from her lips. He rebuked Hannah, but she simply said, "I am pouring my heart out to the LORD. My soul is aching for a child, and I know that the LORD will hear my prayers."

Compassion filled Eli's heart. He told Hannah to go in peace with the assurance that the God of Israel had listened to her prayers and an answer would be forthcoming. And with those encouraging words, the weight of her sorrow lifted from her shoulders. She left the temple and began eating again, her strength restored.

After arriving home, Hannah did conceive and gave birth to the prophet Samuel. She kept her promise to the Lord. After weaning the child at around three years of age, Hannah traveled back to the temple with an offering and returned the child to the Lord, as she had promised.

Every year, Hannah would visit her son in the temple, bringing with her a robe that she had made for him. Not only did the Lord hear her prayers, but she also followed through with the promise she had made to Him.

We see in the story of Hannah an example of consistent and persistent prayer. She yearned for a child and waited patiently for the Lord to answer that prayer. Waiting patiently is the key. We already know that the Lord hears our prayers. Once our prayers leave our hearts and lips, we need to trust the Lord and have patience as we wait for His answer. Lots and lots of patience!

The Bible doesn't state how long Hannah prayed the same prayer; however, we know that her nemesis had numerous sons and daughters. With a typical pregnancy lasting nine months, it could have been upwards of ten to fifteen years.

Hannah was a patient and faithful woman who kept her word. She dedicated Samuel to the Lord. She loved and protected Samuel, and even after she handed him over to Eli, she still loved and protected her child.

If you are a mom, you know that we love and protect our children. We nurture them as infants and toddlers. We put up with their attitudes and body smells when they are teenagers. We provide a roof over their heads and food on the table. We comfort them when they are sad, upset, or hurt. We become mama bears when another child says something to hurt their feelings. We protect them not only from physical harm but also from emotional or mental harm.

Praying for our children is the most loving and protective thing we can do for them. We live in a time when worry trumps trust. We worry about outside influences and what they see on social media, on websites, and in movies. We may discuss our worries with our friends instead of going straight to the Lord in prayer. Please don't misunderstand what I am saying here. It's okay to talk to your friends about your worries, as more than likely they have the same worries too. However, by bringing your concerns and worry to the Lord in prayer, you are handing everything over to Him.

When I started my journey with prayer, I struggled. I didn't know where to begin or even how, but I knew that I needed to. A simple but profound thought occurred to me: If I wasn't praying for my children, who was?

## Reflection and Journal Questions

1. What are some ways that you can commit to time in prayer? Make a list of times that will work best for you and set a reminder on your phone to stop and pray.

2. Have you tried the ACTS way of praying? Which part of the prayer process was easy for you, and what part was the hardest? Why do you think that is?

3. What are some steps you can take to make your prayer time meaningful and entirely focus on the Lord?

4. If you have been reluctant to meditate, has your opinion of meditation changed since it's not at all related to Eastern meditation?

5. Which meditation technique will you be trying and why? Write down the Bible verse that you would like to meditate on and commit to setting aside time to focus on this verse for five days.

6. Studying the Word of God is vital in our spiritual transformations. Which technique: bold-to-bold, writing, outlining it, listening, topical or inductive study, or *lectio divina* would you like to begin

doing? Begin by asking the Lord to reveal which verse or book of the Bible to dive into deeper.

7.  What are some ways that you will incorporate journaling in your life?

8.  Silence and solitude are much needed and beneficial for our walk with Christ. What can you do today to schedule some quiet time with Him? If possible, schedule an extended time from one to twenty-four hours and journal your thoughts, prayers, and whispers the Holy Spirit reveals to you.

9.  Fasting is a spiritual habit that takes willpower and strength. What can you fast from today? Social media? Your favorite food? How will you focus on the Lord through your fasting?

10. Worshiping the Lord can happen anytime and anywhere. What are a few ways that you can worship the Lord today?

11. What part of Hannah's story can you relate to?

# PART 5

## KEEP PRACTICING, KEEP TRANSFORMING

*Create in me a clean heart, O God,*
*and renew a right spirit within me.*
*Cast me not away from your presence,*
*and take not your Holy Spirit from me.*
*Restore to me the joy of your salvation,*
*and uphold me with a willing spirit.*
Psalm 51:10–12

# CHAPTER 22

## GOD LOVES TO TRANSFORM US

*Beloved, we are God's children now,*
*and what we will be has not yet appeared;*
*but we know that when he appears we shall be like him,*
*because we shall see him as he is.*
*And everyone who thus hopes in him*
*purifies himself as he is pure.*
1 John 3:2–3

### The Lord Is the Ultimate Fixer-Upper

Reality TV is big these days. With topics varying from cooking to surviving alone in a remote area to dating and home make-overs, reality TV has us becoming couch potatoes soaking in as much programming as we can.

And now, with streaming services, we can binge-watch our favorite shows. No more waiting until the following week to see a new episode. Now we can just go straight into the next episode, and before you know it, it's way past your intended bedtime. I'm guilty of saying, "Just one more episode, and I'm heading to bed!" When my head finally hits the pillow, I'm exhausted from both the day's events and watching too much TV.

One of the show's that my husband and I like to watch is *Fixer Upper* with Chip and Joanna Gaines. The couple helps homeowners update and repair their homes. Chip and his team go in and demolish everything. When the renovations are complete, Joanna does her thing—decorating the rooms in Farmhouse Chic.

When this show originally aired from 2013 to 2018, Craig and I didn't watch one single episode. We knew about the Gaineses from Waco, Texas, because they are strong in their faith and popular in magazines and interviews.

It wasn't until the spring of 2019 that I became a fan, and my obsession began.

Baylor University is in the heart of Waco, and it was where our oldest had his heart set on attending college. From the moment we set foot on campus, I knew Grant would enroll there. That was a hard pill to swallow because Waco is a fifteen-hour drive from our central Illinois home. After we toured the campus, we drove by the Magnolia Silos and stopped to see what all the fuss was about.

Big mistake!

Now, every time we are in Waco visiting Grant, I need to stop and shop and grab a cupcake and some coffee. All my Mother's Day, birthday, and Christmas gifts are from Magnolia now because Grant can simply go down the road and get a gift for me. I keep telling my family that this is a blessing in disguise because they no longer need to stress about what to get me as a gift. Just get me something, anything from Magnolia.

We watch reruns of *Fixer Upper* on HGTV and the latest episodes on Discovery+. I also want to redesign and paint the interior of our home entirely. Craig hasn't budged on a complete redesign, but he did say that we can discuss repainting the kitchen and dining room. I'll call that a win!

As much as we love watching *Fixer Upper* and the process that a home goes through to get transformed into a habitable living space, I love watching the Lord transform people through spiritual habits.

The Lord is the ultimate Fixer-Upper. He loves flipping His children. He loves to transform us into His image (Genesis 1:27). He loves to demolish the worldly walls around us and replace them with open arms to help and serve others.

He wants us to be the light for Christ. Our Savior Himself spoke of this in Matthew 5:14–16, "You are the light of the world. A city set on a hill cannot be hidden. Nor do people light a lamp and put it under a basket, but on a stand, and it gives light to all in the house. In the same way, let your light shine before others, so that they may see your good works and give glory to your Father who is in heaven."

As you begin practicing spiritual habits, you will be transformed, and people will start to notice. This isn't a quick fixer-upper. Unlike the show, where it takes a few months to transform a house, spiritual transformation is an ongoing process. We will never be perfect or complete, but we will slowly be moving in the direction of Christlikeness.

We will, however, be changed for the better. We will be more conscious of what we do. We will be more attuned to the Holy Spirit. We will know what triggers our sin, and we will step away from those provocations.

We will be a light burning so brightly for Christ that future generations will be talking about the transformation that the Lord did in our lives, and they will want to follow suit.

Our spiritual transformation will benefit future generations.

## Leaving a Spiritual Legacy

Friends, as you practice the spiritual habits consistently, your family and friends will notice it. They will see a woman who wants to leave a spiritual legacy, a woman who puts the Lord first to be the best person she can be.

My Grandma Stauffer left a lasting spiritual legacy for me.

As a child, I would spend weekends or sometimes a whole week on the farm. I can still remember the barn's smell with the dairy cows and the barn cats running around. When it came to milking time, Grandpa

Stauffer would have me get as close to the wall as possible, so I would not get kicked by a cow. I remember the big silver tank that the milk went into and how the milkman would pull his tanker up to collect it.

Grandma Stauffer was the world's best cook. Her chocolate chip cookies were perfect: thin, crispy, and perfectly round. I have her recipe, and I've tried to replicate it. They turned out thick, burned, and rectangular. The same with her peanut butter buckeyes and Christmas cutout cookies. Perfection at its finest! Mine have never, ever turned out like hers. Her cooking skills were not passed down to her granddaughter! But what was passed down was her faith. I think Grandma would agree that this was more important than anything else.

I remember attending vacation Bible school at their church at an early age. Memories of sticking the Bible characters up on the felt, flannel board, singing "Jesus Loves Me," and playing with the shepherd's hook mean VBS to me. There was also a thick, orange crayon that I used every time I colored.

I received my very first Bible from my Grandma Stauffer, and it still sits proudly on my shelf. Throughout my stay on the farm, Grandma and I would drive down the lane to get the mail, work in her garden, eat Schwan's ice cream bars, read stories, and play games. At nighttime, she read the same bedtime stories over and over and stayed with me until I fell asleep.

During my college years, she sent me letters a few times a month with five-dollar bills tucked inside. Her letters continued even after I got married and had the boys. Her penmanship was perfect and never changed throughout the years. In her later years, she gave handmade quilts as gifts for big occasions. I still use the one from my high school graduation, and the ones that we received for our wedding and the birth of the boys are safely put away to be passed down to their children.

## The Most Treasured Letter I Received from Grandma

After my grandpa retired and the farm was too much for them to handle, my grandparents moved into an assisted-living apartment. The

Stauffer family always gathered on Christmas day at noon, and that tradition continued no matter where my grandparents were living.

Grandpa Stauffer always gave us money, and Grandma Stauffer contributed a small gift. A few years before my grandpa passed away, he handed out the usual envelopes, but this time there was more than cash in there. There was a letter from my grandma. And it wasn't just a letter; it was THE letter that I would cherish forever. It is taped in my Bible where I will always see and remember it.

It reads:

> *"Please! Please! Read your Bible. It will tell you what Jesus did for you. Read the book of John & then the last book of the Bible that will tell you what is to come. It will tell you how Jesus came to save you. It will tell if you believe His word & believe in His promises, He will come into your heart & cleanse you from all sin. You must believe in Him with all your heart to do His will. But you must do this before you die. If you will trust Jesus, when you die He will take you home to heaven where you will be with Jesus forever & ever. But if you do not, when you die you will not go to heaven. You will go to the place of torment forever. Please trust Jesus now. He is calling you & please do not turn Him away. He loves you & wants to help you & we love you too & want all our family in heaven."*

My sweet grandma wanted nothing more than for her family, her whole family, to be in heaven with her and grandpa.

Now is the time, friends, to be transformed and not conformed. It's never too late to grow closer to God. He is waiting for you with open arms. Run and embrace Him!

# RESOURCES

Alexander, David, and Pat Alexander. *Zondervan Handbook to the Bible*. Zondervan Pub. House, 2017.

Barton, R. Ruth. *Sacred Rhythms: Arranging Our Lives for Spiritual Transformation*. InterVarsity Press, 2006.

Foster, Richard J. *Celebration of Discipline: The Path to Spiritual Growth*. HarperOne, 2018.

Gower, Ralph. *The New Manners & Customs of Bible Times*. Moody Press, 2005.

*Holy Bible: New Living Translation*. Tyndale House Publishers, Inc., 2015.

Keller, Timothy. *Prayer: Experiencing Awe and Intimacy with God*. Penguin Books, 2016.

Mathis, David. *Habits of Grace*. Crossway, 2016.

Syswerda, Jean E., and Ann Spangler. *Women of the Bible: A One-Year Devotional Study*. Zondervan, 2015.

Whitney, Donald S. *Spiritual Disciplines for the Christian Life*. NavPress, 2014.

## Websites:

Fasting: https://www.thegospelcoalition.org/article/fasting-not-spiritually-elite-hurting/.

Handwriting and memory: https://redbooth.com/blog/handwriting-and-memory

Mediation section: Rephrasing: https://minds-in-bloom.com/teaching-kids-to-paraphrase-step-by-step/

Paul: https://overviewbible.com/apostle-paul/.

# ENDNOTES

**Chapter 2: For Such a Time as This—**
**Why Spiritual Habits are Important**
1 Donald S. Whitney, *Spiritual Disciplines for the Christian Life*.
(Colorado Springs: NavPress, 2014), 4.

**Chapter 10: My First Experience with the Spiritual Habits**
2 Ruth Haley Barton, *Sacred Rhythms: Arranging Our Lives for Spiritual Transformation* (Downers Grove: InterVarsity Press, 2006), 25.

**Chapter 12: Practicing Spiritual Habits**
**Leads to Spiritual Transformation**
3 Barton. *Sacred Rythms: Arranging Our Lives for Spiritual Transformation*, 12.

**Chapter 14: The Spiritual Habit of Prayer**
4 Foster, *Celebration of Discipline: The Path to Spiritual Growth*, 33.
5 Whitney, *Spiritual Disciplines for the Christian Life*, 83.
6 Nicole Pepper, email to author, June 13, 2020.
7 Keller, Timothy. *Prayer: Experiencing Awe and Intimacy with God* (New York: Penguin Books, 2014), 32.

**Chapter 15: The Spiritual Habit of Meditation**

8 Whitney, *Spiritual Disciplines for the Christian Life*, 46

9 Foster, *Celebration of Discipline: The Path to Spiritual Growth*, 21

10 "Teaching Kids to Paraphrase Step by Step" Minds in Bloom, https://minds-in-bloom.com/teaching-kids-to-paraphrase-step-by-step/

**Chapter 16: The Spiritual Habit of Study**

11 Whitney, *Spiritual Disciplines for the Christian Life*, 22.

12 Whitney, *Spiritual Disciplines for the Christian Life*, 28

13 https://redbooth.com/blog/handwriting-and-memory.

14 Barton, *Sacred Rhythms: Arranging Our Lives for Spiritual Transformation*, 54.

**Chapter 17: The Spiritual Habit of Journaling**

15 David Mathis, *Habits of Grace* (Wheaton: Crossway, 2016), 128.

**Chapter 18: The Spiritual Habit of Silence and Solitude**

16 Foster, *Celebration of Discipline: The Path to Spiritual Growth*, 103.

17 Foster, *Celebration of Discipline: The Path to Spiritual Growth*. 102.

**Chapter 19: The Spiritual Habit of Fasting**

18 David Kakish, "Fasting Isn't for the Spiritually Elite". *It's for the Hurting*, January 3, 2020, https://www.thegospelcoalition.org/article/fasting-not-spiritually-elite-hurting/.

19 Whitney, *Spiritual Disciplines for the Christian Life*, 214.

20 Foster, *Celebration of Discipline: The Path to Spiritual Growth*, 60.

**Chapter 20: The Spiritual Habit of Worship**

21 Whitney, *Spiritual Disciplines for the Christian Life*, 103–104.

22 Whitney, *Spiritual Disciplines for the Christian Life*, 104.

# Order Information

To order additional copies of this book, please visit
www.redemption-press.com.
Also available on Amazon.com and BarnesandNoble.com
or by calling toll-free 1-844-2REDEEM.

CPSIA information can be obtained
at www.ICGtesting.com
Printed in the USA
JSHW022255260322
24276JS00003B/25